The Matrimonial Lawyer
A Survival Guide

SECOND EDITION

The Matrimonial Lawyer
A Survival Guide

SECOND EDITION

Imogen Clout MA (Oxon)
Solicitor

ƒℓ Family Law

2001

Family Law is a publishing imprint of
Jordan Publishing Limited
21 St Thomas Street
Bristol BS1 6JS

British Library Cataloguing-in-Publication Data
A catalogue record for this book is available from the British Library.

ISBN 0 85308 736 9

Typeset by Mendip Communications Ltd, Frome, Somerset
Printed and bound in Great Britain by Bell & Bain Ltd, Glasgow

PREFACE TO THE SECOND EDITION

Writing the second edition of this book has been a curious experience in time travel. When I was writing the original edition (published as *The Matrimonial Solicitor – A Guide to Good Practice*), some 11 years ago, my son was a small baby; he is now at secondary school. Other things have changed drastically as well. I feel like the writer of the preface to the *Little Grey Rabbit* books who points out to modern children that of course they must remember that in those days there was no such thing as electricity or water on tap in the kitchen. When I wrote the book, faxes printed onto rolls of special photosensitive paper. They scrolled out of the machines and had to be cut up with scissors and weighted down to stop them rolling up. They faded dramatically in sunlight, so you always sent a letter as well, just in case. A portable phone was portable, in the sense that it could be carried, but you needed another hand or bag to carry it in.

Solicitors entering the profession now may feel that it is inconceivable to imagine life before the fax, the mobile phone, e-mail and the internet. But there was, and many solicitors will probably look back to those days as halcyon, when time ran slower and the demands of quality assurance and franchising were remote.

It is not only technology that has changed. Good practice has become a widely used and recognised term in the legal profession; something that is more than the demands of the *Guide to the Professional Conduct of Solicitors*, something that distinguishes the excellent practitioner from the run-of-the-mill. The Solicitors Family Law Association, of which I was an early member, has done much to promulgate the ethos of good practice not only to its members but, by example, to all family law solicitors. The Legal Aid Board (now the Legal Services Commission) and the courts have also taken active steps to insist on what was advocated as good practice becoming the norm, the industry standard. The Legal Practice Course has also treated skills as a crucial part of a solicitor's education. No one now should be faced with my experience as a young solicitor; during the whole of my articles and the first year post-qualification I never interviewed a client because it was the firm's policy that only partners and senior staff had such face-to-face contact with clients. This meant that at my first meeting with a client, at the firm to which I subsequently moved, I had no real idea of what to do or say. The new firm's senior managing clerk, Ron Hemmings, to whom I owe an undying debt of gratitude, rescued me and gave me a list of things I needed to ask. This was the original germ of the Fact File form and Transaction Pack, aspects of which appear in this book.

However, although the technology and the tenets of good practice have moved on remarkably in the last 10 years, firms and people have not necessarily moved as fast. There are still many firms where family law is not treated as a specialist subject, and there will still be trainees and young solicitors thrown in at the deep end, having to learn 'on the job'. This is a stressful experience and it does not do your clients much good either. This book is intended to meet your needs. I am not writing about 'good practice' as something which is meant for a kite mark or is intended to burden you with another layer of administration. 'Good practice' in this context should help to make your job easier because you become more skilful at it and this should also have the effect of benefiting your clients.

As a last word, some thanks and dedications are in order. I must thank Martin West, my editor, for his encouragement and support, and Alvine Parramore, my domestic goddess, without whose help there would never be enough time to do any writing. And I should like to dedicate the book to my husband, David Body. I fought shy of dedicating the first edition to him because it seemed inappropriate to dedicate a book on divorce to a loving husband. But this is really a book about being a good solicitor, and he is the best I know.

IMOGEN CLOUT
June 2001, Sheffield

CONTENTS

INTRODUCTION

The purpose of this book is not to tell you about divorce and family law; there are plenty of excellent textbooks to help you with that. This book is intended to assist the practitioner who is new to the field of family law or the newly qualified legal adviser, in how best to practise family law.

It is meant as a book of suggestions rather than rules. You may disagree with my suggestions or develop other methods of working. The important thing is to have a clear idea of what you want to achieve and then to design for yourself practical methods of working which suit you best. This book will have succeeded in its purpose if it makes you think about why you are doing what you are doing and how you could improve it.

The overall objective is to be a 'good' matrimonial lawyer: a value judgment which is easier to define by saying what it is not rather than what it is, but I intend to try to say what it is. Indeed, the whole of this book is, in its way, an attempt to put the definition into practice. You should be aiming to be a matrimonial lawyer who is not only respected among professional colleagues but also respected and considered to be good by your clients. Clients will judge you by your attitude to them, your grasp of the law, your resourcefulness and common sense, and your ability to deal with their cases promptly and efficiently.

Technical knowledge of the law is only a small part of being a good matrimonial lawyer. You do not need an encyclopaedic knowledge, but you should be able to identify what it is that you do not know and know where to find it.

You are part of a profession, and professional standards should inform all aspects of your working life. Your client should feel that during the time that you are dealing with his case it is the most important case in hand.

Often, clients who come to see solicitors about family matters are suffering from a crisis in self-esteem, and this adds to their predicament. Part of your task is to build up your client's confidence and, the further it has fallen, the more effort this will require. It is not just a theory that clients are equal before the law; they should be treated as equal by everyone involved in the law, particularly you. This is a fundamental courtesy and is often overlooked.

If you are a good matrimonial lawyer you will quickly build up a reputation. Clients pass on your name to their friends, who pass it on in turn. Clients are not easily fooled. They will know when you take proper care of them, and will resent it if you do not.

Many of the ideas here are counsels of perfection. No one can adhere to them all the time and I would not pretend that I have always done so, but they represent ideals worth striving for. They should help you to work better and more efficiently. This should, in turn, make you and your client more satisfied with what you do, and make your work as a matrimonial lawyer more rewarding.

MOTIVATION

It is not enough just to get on with the business of being a matrimonial lawyer without giving considerable thought to why you do it and how you do it. It is essential that you are conscious of this rather than acting instinctively, so that you can develop a philosophy which informs the whole of your practice.

The main reason for this is that practising family law is stressful. The work which you do is bound up in people's intimate lives at a time when they are going through great trauma. There is a very real danger of being caught up in this emotional turmoil yourself.

To help avoid this, it is a good idea, at an early stage, to be honest with yourself about your motives for choosing to specialise in matrimonial work. If you can identify your own motives you can use this knowledge to protect yourself and stop yourself from developing bad practice habits.

The following are some of the obvious motives of people who practise matrimonial work, any one of which, if allowed free rein, can be detrimental to you or your client.

Helping other people

The desire to help other people is probably the major motive of most matrimonial solicitors, but it is not an easy one to articulate or to admit, partly because, put like this, it sounds patronising, and partly, also, because we are aware of a commonly held view that solicitors often do not do anyone any good. However, the good matrimonial lawyer does help people and can appreciably improve their quality of life and that of their families.

Organising other people

This is a polite way of saying 'bossiness'. We like sorting out other people's problems. It is a large part of any lawyer's role and is not confined to family law.

You have to feel fairly confident before you admit it but, essentially, for the best possible motives, the matrimonial solicitor enjoys trying to set people's lives in order.

Curiosity

People are fascinating, and one of the things which keeps the job interesting is the huge variety of human experience related to you day after day. People and their families can be a never-ending source of interest, amusement, drama and pathos.

In Ian McKellen's show, *Acting Shakespeare,* he challenged the audience to name a happy couple in any one of Shakespeare's plays. It proved an almost impossible task. The point being that domestic bliss is not the stuff of great dramatic interest. There is seldom a dull moment in the life of the matrimonial solicitor (except for preparing lists of documents).

Social awareness

Family law interests other people. At parties it is not a conversation stopper, like admitting that you are a tax lawyer. You deal with issues which touch most people's lives. Everybody has an opinion on divorce and sometimes views are aired with such ferocity that it appears that the speaker regards the rate of marriage breakdown as your personal responsibility. You are likely to be assailed with comment and your opinion will be sought on general and particular issues.

If you have not already formed your own opinions you will need to start reading up on the subject and becoming aware of the tenor of public opinion. It can help to start keeping a scrapbook of press cuttings about the family and family law.

BEWARE OF YOUR MOTIVES

As is probably apparent, any of the motives outlined above could incite behaviour which is not compatible with your status as a professional. Wanting to help people and organise them could incite you to interfere too much in the lives of your clients. You could find yourself trying to take over the way clients run their homes and treat their children. One of the things you have to learn is to stand back and allow your clients to stand back as well. You have done your clients a disservice if they become so dependent on you that they cannot make a move without consulting you first – which can store up trouble for yourself in the future. It can also wear you out. You can run yourself ragged trying to do everything possible for your clients. As their cases proceed you have to encourage them to take the initiative themselves. They can take a frien them to proceedings instead of you. They can be encouraged by you to ring up the authorities themselves. They can be made aware that there are other agencies who can help them without you having abandoned them; make use of such agencies as much as you can.

Curiosity also has its problems. You must not pry into the private lives of your clients just to satisfy your curiosity. Find out only what you need to know for the petition and the affidavits. If your clients want to tell you the minutiae of their married lives you have to bear in mind, on the one hand, that you want to do an efficient job as well as a thorough one, with the possibility, on the other hand, that the clients may feel that they have told you too much which could make the later relationship with them embarrassing for you both.

Social awareness can be dangerous if it leads you to take up an ideological or political stance which clouds your professional judgment. You are not there to judge your clients; you are there to render them the best possible professional service.

The motives which I have outlined above are only by way of example. There are many other influencing factors in your decision to practise as a matrimonial solicitor. The important thing is to spend some time on self-analysis. If you get your own feelings clear, it can help you deal with difficult clients and situations where you have to make decisions of principle. If you become aware of your prejudices you can make an effort not to let them colour the way in which you deal with your clients.

ETHOS: HOW YOU DO IT

There are two aspects of being a good matrimonial lawyer. The first is to be strictly professional, with a high standard of conduct and care for your client. The second is to make a living at it, and this is not to be despised. If you cannot earn sufficient money to enable your firm to run properly, you cannot put into practice your desire to provide a proper service for your client. As I attempt to show in Chapter 13 on costs, the two considerations are not incompatible, and the same professional motives should inform each of them.

However, there is potential conflict between the two considerations. For example, it is fairly obvious that you will start to run up costs much faster if you make the divorce proceedings as acrimonious as possible. If every time a client ⁻ᵗʰ a small grouse you fire off a broadside letter to the other solicitors; ₁ts to fight over trifles via solicitors rather than trying to hemselves; if you encourage applications to court and ₃s; if you send questionnaires which ask about every last pages; if you encourage your client not to be forthcoming ⁻ce the other side to engage in costly applications to force answers; if you refuse to settle your cases, persuading your clients that only the court can give them their 'rights' – if you do all these things you will certainly increase costs enormously and send fat bills to your clients, but you will not necessarily have acted in their best interests at all and, ultimately, your clients will be dissatisfied with the amount you have cost them.

Although the procedural changes that have been introduced to ancillary relief are aimed at curbing the worst excesses of such behaviour, there are undoubtedly some practitioners who do all or many of the things I have mentioned and thereby build up a reputation for being hard and aggressive. There are many clients who think that only this approach can possibly get them what they want. Such practitioners affect to despise the more conciliatory approach, but in most cases such an approach is the best approach for the client. It reduces the acrimony between the parties, it enables them to have a better relationship with each other and any children involved, it settles the case more quickly and it costs the client less. The question of which approach will make the most money for you and your firm is the last factor which should be in your mind when you consider with your clients the strategy which you need to adopt in each particular set of circumstances.

In every aspect of your working life you have to bear in mind that you are a member of a profession. You have to balance your clients' needs, emotional and fiscal, against your need to run a business. If the balance cannot be maintained, you must put your own needs second, because that is what being a member of a profession means. Part of the purpose of this book is to try to suggest ways of becoming efficient and practical in what you do so that these choices do not impose an unbearable strain on your working life.

CODES OF BEHAVIOUR

In the hurly-burly of office life it is easy to lose sight of the ethical basis for what you are doing. From time to time it is a useful exercise to read the Law Society's Guide to Professional Conduct as a refresher. As a matrimonial solicitor you may also find useful the Solicitors Family Law Association (SFLA) code of practice (reproduced at the end of this introduction). This sets out a sensible, attainable standard of professional behaviour. Moreover, if adhered to, it will ensure a way of working which is beneficial to both you and your clients.

However, beware of using the SFLA code as an excuse for not taking positive action, lest this should be interpreted as being too aggressive. This would be a misreading of the code and of the general approach of the SFLA. The conciliatory approach should be the first way of dealing with a case, but there will be cases where the circumstances dictate that you have to act fast and obtain the backing of the court first without pausing to try to negotiate a settlement.

NOT GETTING INVOLVED

Numerous people will tell you that you must not 'get involved' with your clients. This is an oversimplification. You do need to be able to express your sympathy for your clients, but you also need, for their sake and yours, to exercise professional detachment. It is a mistake to empathise and become so bound up in their cases that you cannot stand back from them. It is a skill which comes with time and practice, but you need to work at it, and the ability to be self-analytical, which I mentioned earlier, is particularly important here.

Do not write letters which appear to express your personal feelings, for example: 'we are outraged at your client's disgusting behaviour . . .'. Even if this is how your client feels, you must moderate the language to minimise acrimonious exchanges and repercussions, otherwise there is a danger that the dispute will become so vituperative that communication is scarcely possible. Part of your function is to act as a buffer between the parties, absorbing the worst of their remarks and softening the responses so that dialogue can continue.

KEEPING UP TO DATE

Family law which, at one time, seemed immutable and stable, has changed with startling rapidity in the last few years, even if some of the heralded changes have not been brought into force. It is hard to keep abreast of all the changes that you have to know about and you need to devise a strategy to help you to do this. The internet helps, of course, and services like Lawtel that offer a daily updating service. If your firm subscribes to one of these, make use of it to alert you to what is going on. Also, make a conscious effort to set some time aside on a regular basis to catch up. If you earmark a Friday afternoon, or an evening, each month on which you will go through all the back copies of the *Gazette*, and *Family Law* and any other useful publications, check the HMSO website (www.legislation.hmso.gov.uk) for the latest statutory instruments, and the Family Law updating service on the web (www.familylaw.co.uk/html/family_law_update.html), you can keep it under control. In a firm where there are several family law practitioners you can divide the task up and run regular updating sessions for yourselves. This is useful because it gives you a chance to discuss the practical implications of any changes.

LOOKING AFTER YOURSELF

You need to take care of yourself. Do not let your clients' problems get on top of you. Investigate ways of relieving stress. Take some exercise, or spend some time doing an activity as different from work as possible. Take a break at lunchtime and, even if only briefly, leave the office and get some fresh air. Take proper breaks during the day for tea or coffee. Learn relaxation techniques. These may not seem relevant in a book about the matrimonial lawyer but should not be underestimated. They are important to help ensure that you have the energy and enthusiasm to carry out your work efficiently.

A BRIEF NOTE ON GENDER

In writing this book I had to face the dilemma of which gender to use for the client. I have solved it by using 'he' or 'she' indiscriminately as the mood has taken me for both clients and their lawyers.

CODE OF PRACTICE FOR SFLA MEMBERS

GENERAL

1. At an early stage, you should explain to your client the approach you adopt in family law work.

2. You should encourage your client to see the advantages to the family of a constructive and non-confrontational approach as a way of resolving differences. You should advise, negotiate and conduct matters so as to help the family members settle their differences as quickly as possible and reach agreement, while allowing them time to reflect, consider and come to terms with their new situation.

3. You should make sure that your client understands that the best interests of the child should be put first. You should explain that where a child is involved, your client's attitude to the other family members will affect the family as a whole and the child's relationship with his or her parents.

4. You should encourage the attitude that a family dispute is not a contest in which there is a winner and a loser, but rather that it is a search for fair solutions. You should avoid using words or phrases that suggest or cause a dispute where there is no serious dispute.

5. Emotions are often intense in family disputes. You should avoid inflaming them in any way.

6. You should take great care when considering the effect your correspondence could have on other family members and your own client. Your letters should be clearly understandable and free of jargon. Remember that clients may see assertive letters between solicitors as aggressive declarations of war. Your correspondence should aim to resolve issues and to settle the matter, not to further inflame emotions or to antagonise.

7. You should stress the need for your client to be open and honest in all aspects of the case. You must explain what could happen if your client is not open and honest.

RELATIONSHIP WITH A CLIENT

8. You should make sure that you are objective and do not allow your own emotions or personal opinions to influence your advice.

9. You must give advice and explain all options to your client. The client must understand the consequences of any decisions that he or she has to make. The decision is to be made by your client, you cannot decide for your client.

10. You must make your client aware of the legal costs at all stages. The benefits and merits of any step must be balanced against the costs.

11. You should make sure that your client knows about other available services (such as mediation and counselling) which may bring about a settlement, help your client and other family members, or both. You should explore, with your client, the possibility of reconciliation and, where appropriate, give every encouragement.

DEALING WITH OTHER SOLICITORS

12. In all dealings with other solicitors, you should show courtesy and try to maintain a good working relationship.

13. You should try to avoid criticising the other solicitors involved in a case.

DEALING WITH A PERSON WHO DOES NOT HAVE A SOLICITOR

14. When you are dealing with someone who is not represented by a solicitor, you should take even greater care to communicate clearly and try to avoid any technical language or jargon, which is not easily understood.

15. You should strongly recommend an unrepresented person to consult an SFLA solicitor in the interests of the family.

COURT PROCEEDINGS

16. When taking any step in the proceedings, the long-term effect on your client and other family members must be balanced with the likely short-term benefit to the case.

17. If the purpose of taking a particular step in proceedings may be misunderstood or appear hostile, you should consider explaining it, as soon as possible, to the others involved in the case.

18. Before filing a petition, you and your client should consider whether the other party or his or her solicitor should be contacted in advance about the petition, the 'facts' on which the petition is to be based and the particulars, with a view to coming to an agreement and minimising misunderstandings.

19. When you or your client receive a Petition or Statement of Arrangements for approval, unless there are exceptional circumstances, you should advise your client not to start his or her own proceedings without giving the other party at least 7 days' notice, in writing, of the intention to do so.

20. You should discourage your client from naming a co-respondent unless there are very good reasons to do so.

CHILDREN

21. You should encourage both your client and other family members to put the child's welfare first.

22. You should encourage parents to co-operate when making decisions concerning the child, and advise parents that it is often better to make arrangements for the child between themselves, through their solicitors or through a mediator, rather than through a court hearing.

23. In any letters you write, you should keep disputes about arrangements for the child separate from disputes about money. They should usually be referred to in separate letters.

24. You must remember that the interests of the child may not reflect those of either parent. In exceptional cases it may be appropriate for the child to be represented separately by the Official Solicitor, a panel guardian (in specified proceedings) or, in the case of a 'mature' child, by another solicitor.

WHEN THE CLIENT IS A CHILD

25. You should only accept instructions from a child if you have the necessary training and expertise in this field.

26. You must continually assess the child's ability to give instructions.

27. You should make sure that the child has enough information to make informed decisions. The solicitor should advise and give information in a clear and understandable way and be aware that certain information may be harmful to the child.

28. You should not show favour towards either parent, the local authority or any other person involved in the court proceedings.

29.   Detailed guidelines for solicitors acting for children have been drawn up by the SFLA. Copies are available from the address below.

If you would like a list of local SFLA members please send a stamped addressed envelope to:

Mary I'Anson
Administrative Director
SFLA
PO Box 302
Orpington BR6 8QX

For more details, telephone 01689 850227.

Chapter 1

MAKING THE FIRST CONTACT

Your client will gain his first impression of you and the firm where you work when he walks into reception or rings up to make an appointment. It is important that this first impression has the right effect on your client, confirming his decision to consult you and making him feel confident that you are the best person to act for him. There is a lot you can do to influence the impact first contact will make, even if you are not in a position of very much authority in the firm.

TELEPHONE CONTACT

Try ringing up your office sometime. Is the phone answered promptly? Does the person who answers it say the name of the firm distinctly? Some solicitors' offices just say 'Hello' which is rather disconcerting, some play awful music when they put you on hold. (A local estate agent I know plays 'Home on the Range' which always reduces me to giggles by the time I speak to the person I want.) Does the person answering the phone sound friendly? If you think that the impression given is off-putting, see what you can do to change things by mentioning your experiences to the partner in charge.

WHEN THE CLIENT WALKS IN

What does your reception area look like? Bring what influence you can to bear to make it look clean, tidy, efficient and welcoming. (The same criteria apply to the receptionist!) Is there some provision for children, such as a box of toys, or picture books? You may feel that it is better if clients do not bring children, but some have no choice, and it is better if they feel provided for, rather than resented.

VETTING THE CLIENT

This is a task which preferably should not be delegated. It is less trouble in the long run if you speak personally to the potential client who phones you. You can judge for yourself whether your client has a real problem and whether it is within your power to do anything about it. After all, the client may have been put through to you because he told the receptionist that it was a 'family problem'. It may only then become apparent that it is really to do with inheritance and probate, and the client should be referred to one of your colleagues. Speaking to the client yourself helps you to distinguish between the casual inquirer and the person who wants a long session of advice. Some matters can even be dealt with in that first phone call.

Some practitioners take the view that you ought always to arrange for the client to come in to the office rather than go into detail on the phone. This ensures that the client can sign a Legal Help Form, even if he never calls again. You have to balance this against the administrative time and cost of opening a file and submitting the Legal Help Form for payment. For my part, I think that there is no harm in being generous with advice on the phone if you can deal with a matter fairly briefly. Potential clients are generally grateful and may well come back to you later if the problem does not resolve itself. They may even recommend you to one of their friends.

Speaking to the client yourself also helps you to prepare for the first interview. You can decide whether there is a real emergency or whether the urgency is only in the mind of your client, and make an appropriate appointment. If it becomes apparent that there is a legal point at issue which is not within your detailed grasp – recognition of foreign decrees, for instance – you can look it up before the meeting and be in a better position to advise.

You can also assess whether the client or the case is going to be a 'problem'. For instance, not every client who rings up wanting to change solicitors is going to be 'difficult', but some certainly are. There are no easy guidelines. Only experience will teach you the danger signs. I now know that I should really have spotted in advance the woman who said that she wanted to change from her present solicitors because they were writing to her husband's solicitors. When I got the papers I found, with a sinking heart, that I was the sixth solicitor she had consulted and it was not long before she was seeking number seven!

However, not all clients who sound odd or who are aggrieved with their present solicitors are problem cases. Some of the horror stories about the way people have been represented are true. Some clients who may cause your heart to sink when you first encounter them by phone are perfectly straightforward face to face.

If you are in doubt, consider agreeing to a diagnostic interview; it will not commit you to acting, but will give the client a chance to explain the problem fully. If your client is already publicly funded you will need to think about how to fund the case because, if you do not subsequently take on the client, you cannot seek authority for the client to sign another Legal Help Form. Consequently, you may need to consider asking for a flat fee to cover it. In the case of a private client, this is a problem which should not arise, but you should explain in advance your hourly rate of charge and agree on payment to avoid any later misunderstanding.

If you cannot take on the client, or choose not to do so, do not simply abandon him. Suggest another firm or advice agency which the client might approach. If you do not, it looks as though you do not care, and this attitude reflects badly on the profession as a whole.

ASKING YOUR SECRETARY TO VET CLIENTS

If you are unable to speak to the potential client when he phones, then, if possible, your own secretary should do so. Brief her on what you will want her to find out. Explain the sorts of things you want to know and why you think they are important. One of my secretaries and I worked out a form which she could fill in when a client rang up and which provided basic information so that I was forewarned before the first appointment. When she was away these blank forms were given to the temp and the receptionist. There is a specimen form at Appendix 1A to this chapter.

APPOINTMENTS

Try to see the client as soon as possible. If you do not, you run the risk of losing the client altogether, as matrimonial clients often have to screw up their courage enormously to approach a lawyer and, if you do not respond promptly, they can get 'cold feet'. Sometimes, urgent action is needed, but you do not always find out about this in your first conversation with your client because clients do not always realise when something is urgent. Every solicitor has experienced the client who pulls out a much crumpled piece of paper which indicates that legal action needs to be taken that day, or should have been taken the day before.

There is a high drop-out rate for first appointments, even where you have arranged to see the client as soon as possible. There is not much that you can do to reduce this. However, appointment cards, like those hospitals use, are helpful. They can look like this:

ANY FIRM & CO
9 THE HIGH STREET
ELSEWHERE TOWN
TELEPHONE 000 00000

Your appointment is with M .... at ...... o'clock
on .... day .... 200.....
If you cannot attend please telephone to let us know.

On the back of such a card you might consider putting any useful publicity, such as a list of the work the firm undertaken by and the people who deal with each subject. You should not make it into a postcard because if you send it to your client without an envelope someone else in his house could read it. Such cards are of most use to the drop-in inquirer, but you can also send them to clients if there is enough time before their appointment. You can also use the cards to confirm arrangements for appointments with existing clients, as well as new ones.

QUESTIONNAIRES IN ADVANCE

Some solicitors send their clients a questionnaire before they see them, the idea being that the client turns up with all the information neatly docketed, which saves time at the first interview. I have never found this very successful. You have to take time anyway to go through the form to ensure that they have completed it correctly. It is very hard to design a questionnaire which is easily answered and most people are bad at filling in forms. I prefer to fill out any such form with the client so as to make sure I have understood everything correctly.

Instead of a questionnaire, it can be helpful to let the client know the sort of information you will need to find out at the first interview and the documents you may need to see, such as:

- recent payslips;
- National Insurance number;
- marriage certificate;
- dates of birth of the children.

I would use this with discretion. There may be a danger in making this list too long so that the client feels overburdened by the first contact. Most of the information you will eventually need can, after all, be supplied at a later stage and you really only need to verify the information for the Legal Help Form the first time you see the client.

SUMMARY

- First impressions are tremendously important.
- Telephone contact is most effective if it is personal.
- Make a list of the primary information that you want.
- Make appointments as soon as possible.
- Use questionnaires carefully.

APPENDIX 1A

TELEPHONE ATTENDANCE SHEET: NEW MATRIMONIAL/FAMILY CLIENTS

Please find out the following information:–

Name..

Address..

....

Daytime telephone number..

Married/cohabiting?

Living together/separated?

Children? ....

Number... Ages ....

Is client working?... (ask client to bring last payslip)

What does s/he do? ....

Please note down the problem briefly

....

....

....

....

....

....

....

....

Did anyone refer client to us?

If so, who? ....

Date .... Time ..... Initials .....

Chapter 2

THE FIRST INTERVIEW

When I originally wrote this chapter, solicitors were not taught how to interview clients. The Legal Practice Course (LPC) has, quite properly, changed that, so you are unlikely to have come to matrimonial law, as I did, with no experience of seeing a client. However, you are unlikely to have been taught to interview in a matrimonial context as it does not form part of the 'core' areas of the LPC. Nor will the practices and assessments have prepared you for a long interview, which is what you will generally need. It is appropriate therefore to consider the subject again, and specifically in the family law context.

The first interview is of crucial importance because it has so many functions for you and for the client.

- It introduces you to each other.
- It enables you to 'sell' yourself and your expertise to your client.
- It allows you to gather information, which enables you to advise, plan a strategy for the future and set the tone.

In order to make the best use of the limited time available, you need to have a clear plan in your head – a hidden agenda. You also need to relax your client so that she is ready to talk freely about matters of some intimacy.

LENGTH OF INTERVIEW

How long should you allow? An hour seems to be the classic length, but do not cram each appointment so tightly that you do not have at least half an hour's leeway. You may have gathered from the initial telephone call with your client whether she is likely to be prolix or whether the matter is so complex that you ought to allocate more time.

I think that most clients find an hour quite long enough and tend to get rather tired by the end of it (so will you). You must avoid making the client feel that she is rushed. On the other hand, you may in some rare cases have to signal that the interview is over by standing up and starting to usher out the client, as politely as possible.

YOUR ROOM

Stand at the door of your room, or the room you are going to use for the interview. Try to see it with the eyes of a stranger – a stranger who is feeling very nervous and uncomfortable, who may never have seen a solicitor's office before. Is it tidy? Does it look efficient? Is the desk cluttered with paper and a pile of teetering files? Is the floor clean? Is the room welcoming?

Small touches make a big difference. If you are going to sit behind a desk, clear it of everything except the things you need for the interview. Your client needs the space to put her elbows on, and spread out any papers. She should not have to talk to you over a barrier.

Do not leave other people's files around for her to see. Most clients are very concerned about confidentiality, and if they see other people's papers around they may worry about what you will do with theirs.

Tidy the room so you look efficient and not harassed. Fresh flowers and cheerful posters or pictures make a very good impression and need not be expensive. Think about the personal things you have around you and the impression they give. Are photographs of your family helpful (because they make you seem human), or off-putting (because you look part of a smugly happy family unit, in contrast to your client's difficulties)?

DO NOT ALLOW INTERRUPTIONS

Stop all incoming calls. Put an engaged sign up, if you have one. You can ruin a gently built-up rapport if you are interrupted because the client stops feeling the centre of your attention.

For the next hour your client needs to feel that she is the centre of your world and all your attention is given to her.

WHERE WILL YOU SIT?

Once in a while, sit in the client's chair to see if it is comfortable? It should be if you are asking her to sit there for an hour or so and bare her soul. Make sure that any light does not shine in her face unpleasantly.

Think about the other furniture. A desk is handy for you; you can spread all your papers on it and it is your home. Behind it you feel safe and authoritative. The desk may confer on you the authority your client wants to see and which she wants you to exercise on her behalf. But your client may also find it off-putting and it may act as a barrier between you. One useful solution is to stay at your desk, but have your client comfortably to the side of it so that you can turn to her but still have something to rest on for writing or use your computer.

Some people favour two armchairs and a coffee table, with a clipboard to hold their papers. This can be nice and comforting for both you and your client, but not many offices have such facilities or enough space in each room. If you are going to do this, make sure that the chairs are comfortable. It is awkward if the two of you are perched on high, dining-type chairs with nowhere to put your knees or lean on comfortably.

The worst scenario is the huge boardroom table, glaringly lit, with the two of you tucked round one corner, or facing each other across the great wooden expanse. This is how many firms have designed their meeting rooms, with the corporate client in mind, but they should be urged to think about how it feels for the private client, who may well be intimidated by the corporate trappings. An unfriendly room can often be made better just by changing the lighting, and this is a fairly cheap solution.

WHEN YOUR CLIENT ARRIVES

Try not to keep your client waiting, even if she is too early. She may be nervous. Most people are frightened of seeing a lawyer – something which came as a surprise to me when I first realised it. But for many people it is as intimidating as going to the dentist, and the longer your client waits, the worse she is likely to feel. Some clients, however, are so nervous that they arrive far too early, 30 minutes or even an hour. You must then decide whether you can see your client or whether it is going to disrupt your carefully planned day; in any case, you may well be in another meeting when she arrives. In this situation, you must enlist the help of your secretary or receptionist and ask her to explain to the client that she is early, and that you will see her as soon as possible. Meanwhile, your client should be offered a cup of tea or coffee and a magazine or newspaper to help pass the time.

MEETING THE CLIENT

When you come face to face, greet your client warmly, and formally. I would never call a client by his or her first name on first acquaintance, and, generally, do not think it is a good idea to be on first name terms. Introduce yourself so he knows that you are the person he has come to see. This is particularly important for the female solicitor who may be mistaken for her own secretary, no matter how professional she looks (which is most deflating to your ego and disconcerting for the client). You may need to practise saying your own name clearly. Many people tend to mumble their names, which makes it rather embarrassing for the client who may feel awkward about asking you to repeat it.

Make a little fuss of the client. Be sure that he is sitting comfortably, has taken off his coat (which you will carefully hang up for him), and has tea or coffee or a glass of water. Offer him a biscuit. Pamper your client.

CHILDREN

If yours is the sort of practice where people come in laden with children, it is as well to have available soft toys, some crayons and paper – old office stationery does very well. This sometimes saves other bits of your office being ravaged. If possible, try to suggest that people do not bring their children, but remember that for some of your clients there is no practical alternative.

Many clients do not think that their children understand what is going on in the interview, and you may need to explain to them that children who cannot talk properly can still understand what is being said and may well be upset by what you are going to have to talk about. Neither of you is going to be able to concentrate properly if small children are not happy and quiet. Sometimes you can get your secretary/receptionist/trainee to help.

If the child is 3 years old or more and has to be in the room, I usually explain my disquiet at discussing anything in detail, give brief advice and encourage the client to make another appointment as soon as possible so that we can discuss her case in privacy. You will have to play such situations by ear.

WHEN THE CLIENT BRINGS A FRIEND

My heart sinks when this occurs because it can make your job extremely difficult. Part of the problem is the feeling of being watched, which can make you acutely self-conscious, and cause you to perform at less than your best.

The first difficulty is that you do not know the nature of your client's relationship with the 'friend'. Does the 'friend' have a benign or baleful influence over her? Is this person egging her on to get a divorce? Is he the potential co-respondent? Is he an interfering relative? Is he a 'barrack-room lawyer'? One of my clients was accompanied to every interview by her father, and I was never sure to what extent she was acting of her own free will and was unable to clarify the matter in his presence. Parents who accompany their adult children can be especially difficult because their natural instinct to protect (and, sometimes, control) their child makes them want to take an active part in the interview.

I try to see my client alone, at least for the first interview, but you cannot make this an absolute rule. You have to judge whether, without the companion, your client will be reduced to a jelly who cannot cope, despite your friendly and supportive approach.

If you discuss the problem with your receptionist, she can warn you when your client turns up escorted. My method of dealing with this eventuality is to go out to the reception and greet the client and ask her to come to my room. If the friend then stands up too and makes as if to accompany her, I generally say to the client that I would really like to see her alone at first and smile cheerfully at the friend. If this does not work I give in and try to mask my feelings. There is no point in starting off the relationship with a tussle of wills. Later in the interview, once you have convinced your client that you do not intend to eat her, you may be able to indicate to her that there are things you need to talk over with her privately and then ask the friend to excuse you. For instance, you do not want to put your client on the spot about her intentions towards a man with whom she has run off and who has accompanied her. You are unlikely to receive a frank answer in his presence.

A real difficulty arises if the friend starts to take over the interview and ask all the questions or, worse, answers them for the client. Then you must take firm control over the interview and stress the private and exclusive nature of the solicitor/client relationship. You also have to be careful about this later on when the friend may ring up for a progress report. Unless your client has specifically authorised you to tell the other person something, you must not do so, but it is easy to get trapped into revealing more than you really should by the knowledge that the caller already has inside information.

OTHER PEOPLE SITTING IN

You may want to have someone else sit in on the first meeting, such as your assistant or trainee. Your client has a right to know who that person is and whether he is helping you or merely listening in as part of his training. Make this clear. Ask the client's permission, putting this in such a way as to make it clear that you feel it would be best if your colleague stayed.

Consider where your colleague should sit. If you sit side-by-side, this is rather intimidating, like an interview panel. It may be preferable for your colleague to sit to one side and slightly behind the client so that he is not a distraction to your client. Sometimes, however this can be fatal, if the client is unintentionally funny and you catch your colleague's eye ...

Establish with your colleague, before the interview, what each of you is going to do. Is he going to write the notes, while you ask the questions? Is he going to run through the basic questions and then let you do the general talking? Do explain to the client if your colleague is going to have the conduct of the file even though you are running the first interview, and explain the limits of your involvement.

STRUCTURE OF THE INTERVIEW

Opening remarks

Once you have settled the client comfortably it is helpful to start the interview by briefly running through what you already know. You should have some information already from your or your secretary's first contact with the client. If the client comes to you 'cold', start by asking him to give you a *brief* outline of why he has come. Most clients are able to summarise their situation, but some will launch straight into the detail of the story, which is not what you want at this stage. This is a waste of time for you both, so you need to keep your client to the point if you can.

Setting an agenda

Once you have the gist of the problem you need to explain how the interview is going to be structured. A good interview needs to be efficient, in the sense that the time needs to be spent profitably. However, your idea of what this means and the client's preconceptions may not necessarily be the same. You will want to gather information that allows you to formulate your 'theory of the case', and to give appropriate advice. Your client may want an opportunity to pour her heart out and find a sympathetic champion who can tell her that it will be all right. These are not necessarily incompatible ideas but they need careful management, which is why you need to have a clear notion of the agenda for the meeting. At the beginning of the chapter, I called this a 'hidden agenda', which it is in the sense that it is not written down and it is flexible, but I do not think that you should conceal it from the client.

It is positively helpful to outline to the client what you propose to do. Most first interviews can follow this broad outline:

- fact-gathering:
    - basic details; and
    - the story of the marriage;
- advice giving:
    - procedure;
    - outcomes;
    - options;
    - costs;
- decisions about what to do next;
- immediate actions to be taken by client and lawyer.

I do not think that you need to be very formal about this. You can say something like: 'Let me tell you what I should like to do this morning. I need to find out a whole lot of details about your marriage and the family. Once I have the full picture then I can give you some advice and you can think about what you would like to do next. And then we can work out what you and I will need to do'.

Not only does this serve as an active reminder to you, which you may need at the early stages of your career, but it lets the client see what is going to happen. If she shows a tendency to ramble and get off the point, or demand advice before you are ready or able to give it, it allows you to steer her back without appearing to be rude or dismissive of her concerns.

Starting to gather information

You then need to move to the fact-gathering part of the interview, and you will be aware that you can use both open and closed questions to elicit a story from a client. Those who have been taught interviewing on the Legal Practice Course will recall that there was a good deal of pressure to avoid the use of closed questions and a checklist. Since many suggestions of how to run a successful interview may seem to contradict that, a little explanation is necessary.

Students who come to interviewing for the first time tend, out of nervousness, to rely heavily on direct questions and checklists because they worry that they will not ask all the necessary questions and therefore will be penalised for not having got the whole story from the client. They regard an interview as a *fact-transferring* exercise. But an interview is much more than this. Therefore, in teaching interviewing skills, emphasis is placed on the skilful use of open questions to get the client to talk and encourage the student to listen *actively*. The problem with the checklist, at this stage, is that it prevents the student from hearing the actual answer given by the client and following up the leads that answer suggests. It promotes a kind of blinkered narrow thinking, rather than an active response to what the client says.

However, in the context of the matrimonial interview, you need a considerable amount of hard fact from the client. If you have a Legal Services Commission (LSC) franchise you have to comply with the transaction criteria and demonstrate that you have asked for all the required information. It is enormously helpful if everyone in the department uses the same method of fact-gathering so that files are consistent and can easily be assimilated by other fee-earners. For all these reasons a checklist is helpful.

Over my years in practice I have developed a form which I call my Fact File (see Appendix 2A). This has all the basic information on it for drafting a petition or filling in Community Law Service (CLS) forms. I explain to my client at the outset that this is my own form, not an official one – in case clients are worried about this, and that once I have asked them for the information covered by it we need not go over it again. I then run through the questions on the form.

Whatever method you adopt to gather this basic information, you need to try to let the exchange evolve like a conversation, not an interrogation. Once you are familiar with the content of your own checklist you can let the questions come naturally while writing the answer as you ask the next question. You can interpolate friendly bits of conversation, such as comments on the names of your client's children, or telling the client a bit about yourself: for example, 'Oh, you got married in Liverpool, that's where my mother comes from'. You can fill in some of the form later. You do not have to follow the form slavishly; the boxes are there to prompt you, not to be read out to the client. For instance, you should not simply ask the client 'Are your children children of the family?', because you cannot expect your client to know the technical definition. You should instead establish, for example, from her description of the children's relationship with their stepfather, whether or not they are children of the family.

You must not assume that your client will know why you are asking the questions. I once completed a form with a client and was talking about her relationship with her husband, when she suddenly said 'I never should have married him again'. When I asked why she had not mentioned this before, she pointed out, quite rightly, that I had not asked her.

Sometimes your client will be tight-lipped in giving the answers, but often a routine question from you will prompt a remark which adds to your picture of the client or the marriage. It is a mistake to try to restrict your client to the matters on the form, but some clients will whizz off into irrelevant areas and need to be brought back to your inquiry. The form can be particularly useful in such situations, as it enables you to bring your client back to the point without appearing hard or unfeeling. Some remark such as 'Can we talk about that in a little while and finish dealing with this now?' generally gets you back to your inquiry.

Getting the client's story

By the time you have completed the form, your client should have concluded that solicitors are not as frightening as she had supposed, and she should be prepared to talk generally. I sometimes use a prefatory remark such as 'Now tell me why things are so difficult between you and your husband'. Some clients need more prompting or coaxing than others; with some, a single question opens the floodgates and you end up with several pages of notes. It is in this part of the interview that open questions may prove to be the most useful, as they prompt the client to talk more freely.

Taking a proof

If a client is seeking an injunction and there are many incidents of violence, or you are dealing with a sequence of 'unreasonable behaviour', it generally seems to be best to ask her to describe the most recent incident first and then work backwards in time. This seems to make the sequence easier to recall. Very few clients, even intelligent, educated ones, are good at putting together a coherent chronological account of events.

When taking a proof of evidence (which is effectively what you are doing as you sit and scribble fiercely whilst the client talks) try to be alert to your client's rhythms of speech and vocabulary. You may have to draft an affidavit or particulars of behaviour from your notes, and it does not help your client if you use words she is not familiar with. It may lead to embarrassment if your client comes to give evidence and does not understand her own affidavit when it is read back to her!

SEX

As sexual problems lie at the root of many matrimonial problems you may well have to discuss them with your client in some detail. If you are dealing with a nullity case, which hinges on non-consummation, you will certainly have to go into intimate detail. This can be particularly embarrassing when you are new to the work, or when you are young and perhaps not very sexually experienced yourself. It helps to remember that your client is likely to be far more embarrassed than you are. I have found that if you are direct and approach the problem straightforwardly it becomes much easier. Use proper terms, rather than coy euphemisms which your client may not understand.

In some cases, you may feel that it would be more productive and make your client feel less embarrassed if a colleague of the same sex as your client takes a note of the relevant details. If so, consult your client first. I once had to interview a young man who had not been able to consummate his marriage. He was reduced to tongue-tied silence and, despite my feeling that I ought to be firm and direct with him, I found that it was more than I could do to ask about the details of penetration. I asked him if he would prefer to talk to my older male colleague. He was plainly relieved by the suggestion so my colleague dealt with that aspect of the matter and my client and I were able to proceed well subsequently.

TISSUES

Tissues are invaluable and essential in my experience. If a client becomes tearful, the worst thing from her point of view, and perhaps worse if the client is a man, is the embarrassment they feel. If you stop trying to ignore it tactfully and, instead, offer the box of tissues quickly saying 'Oh, don't worry, have a tissue', they seem to get over their embarrassment. You are giving your client permission to cry and this stops her feeling so bad about it.

WHAT DOES YOUR CLIENT REALLY WANT?

Once you have the detailed information on the form and the necessary background information, the focus turns to you and your magical problem-solving powers. Before you begin your recital about divorce and how it works, however, you need to find out one more vital thing: what does your client want? You must not make assumptions. You may think that 'with a wife like that' your client must want a divorce, but it is not necessarily so. It is not for you to push your client in that direction. You have a duty to consider with your client whether the marriage can be saved by effecting a reconciliation and you should think about putting your client in touch with agencies which can help. Canvass the options with the client and consider whether legal action is appropriate; if so, consider what sort of action you should bring.

It also helps, if divorce or separation is what your client wants, to find out what sort of financial settlement she has in mind. People are often constrained by their preconceptions of what divorce courts order. Friends and the popular press can leave people with a most distorted view of the law. A good way to find out your client's real feelings is to ask her to forget what she thinks the likely outcome will be and to imagine what she would choose if a fairy with a magic wand granted her a wish. Her wish may be totally unrealistic, but at least it gives you an idea of what she wants; for example, how she feels about staying in the house or about a clean break. You can then use this as a basis for the advice you give, and it may guide you as to how readily that advice will be accepted.

Clients may also need advice about other issues: welfare benefits (because of franchising requirements) and tax are the obvious ones, and you may need to mention others, such as housing, or wills. Some clients may need this information even more than divorce advice, if they are still at the stage of considering what options are open to them. This is a lot of information for a client to take in at one session, on top of all the basic divorce and separation information that you need to give. You need to consider the best strategy for conveying all these points. You can touch on the advice during the interview and write about it in more detail in letters to the client. (If you decide to do this you need to make sure that you do follow up the advice, perhaps by ticking it off on a checklist.) Some clients will be happy to be given information leaflets and go away and digest them at leisure. Clients who are not comfortable with the written word will not find either approach enormously helpful, however. For such clients you can sometimes arrange a shorter follow-up appointment to discuss these particular issues.

GIVING ADVICE

Tell your client clearly what he can do and what is likely to happen, using simple language; 'ancillary relief' is too technical a term to be of any use to the layman.

If a divorce is in prospect, your client will need to know the various stages of the procedure, but it is complicated and a great deal to take in at this first meeting. Consider whether it would be better to write your client a long letter setting it out clearly (you can design a standard letter for this) or prepare an explanatory sheet (see Appendix 2B) which your client can keep for reference.

Be realistic, both about time and about quantum. It may be fair to say that an undefended divorce, with both parties co-operating, will generally take between four and six months, but this depends on your local court and how quickly the solicitors on both sides operate. You need to explain the factors which influence the length of time it will take. If you underestimate, you run the risk of an angry client who thinks that you are inefficient and tells other people so.

QUANTUM

Each lawyer has his or her own personal style. Some are very 'bullish' and talk up the amounts they think that their client will obtain. This is fine if you are confident of success, and you may end up with your client leaving the first interview feeling cheerful because you have advised her that she will be better off than she expected. On the other hand, you risk disappointing your client because the settlement falls short of the expectation you have created. You can, of course, take another line and underestimate a little in order to be on the safe side. A better course is to talk about the principles involved in determining the share each party will have, so that your client can understand the deciding factors, such as the welfare of the children, the wife's reasonable needs, the 'yardstick of equality' and what 'reasonable' means in this context.

It can be helpful to have the factors the court takes into account, as set out in s 25 of the Matrimonial Causes Act 1973, printed out on a separate sheet that you can give to clients for later reference. Not all clients will find this helpful, and it may be information overload to give this out at the first meeting, but it is useful in some cases.

It is important to explain to your client that when you refer to the court you are using a form of shorthand and that the court is the last resort. You need to explain that you would hope to settle the case out of court, but that your client must bear in mind what the court would be likely to order if the matter was fought, and the costs which would then be involved.

THINKING TIME

Your client may already have decided what she wants to do, or may be able to decide immediately after you have given your advice. But avoid pushing for a decision if your client needs time to make a rational choice. Even in what you perceive as an emergency, you should impress upon your client what the consequences of delay will be, but she must still be allowed to delay if she chooses. Time and again, people who have experienced divorce and family law procedures complain that they were whisked along and felt that they had no control over the proceedings once they had started. You do not want to put your client in that position.

On the other hand, you do not want to let the whole matter go dead. Litigation needs momentum in order to be successful, and you must keep it going. One of the best ways of balancing these needs is to send the client who thinks that she probably wants to initiate proceedings, a draft letter to her husband for her to consider. In this way, you can check that the letter will strike the right tone and it gives your client control over the speed and tenor of the action. Sometimes your client will come straight back to you; sometimes she may consider the position for several weeks as she weighs up the pros and cons of your advice and thinks about giving her husband a second chance.

If you need to produce a speedy reply, for example, to a letter before action, you may need to dictate (or draft on screen) a reply while your client is with you, rather than let the matter wait until a draft has been sent to her and she has approved it. This is a procedure which always makes me feel acutely self-conscious and I inevitably drop the microphone and forget what all the buttons are for – but clients do appreciate the involvement it gives them.

COSTS

I have devoted a separate chapter to this area because of its importance. You must deal with it at the first meeting so that you and your client make a contract for the services you will supply. Your firm will almost certainly have a standard procedure that you have to adopt. Asking for money is embarrassing, but you should use a direct and straightforward approach. Your aim is to make the basis of your charges clear to your client so that she knows where she stands. This is just as important as making the legal issues clear.

GETTING FORMS SIGNED

If your client is publicly funded, it is a good idea to get as many forms as possible completed and signed at the first interview. This saves the time spent sending them to the client later and the attendant costs. Appropriate forms may be all or any of the following:

- public funding application forms;
- emergency funding form;
- petition form (where the basis for the petition is clear);
- statement of arrangements for the children;
- application for exemption from fees.

You can also have a small stock of standard letters your client can sign if necessary such as a letter from your client to her previous solicitors asking them to send their papers to you, or a letter to your client's doctor authorising a report to be sent to you.

ENDING THE INTERVIEW

Establish clearly with your client what the next steps are, what you will be doing and what you expect her to do.

Give your client your card. Tell her who she should speak to if you are not available. It helps to impress upon your client that your secretary can be safely trusted to take a message (if indeed she can) and may be able to offer some assistance. If you have an assistant who will be looking after the file, introduce him to your client.

Indicate to your client when your next meeting together might be. If you are dealing with an emergency remedy you may need to make a definite appointment to deal with the next stage of the proceedings.

AFTERMATH

If possible, dictate a note of the interview instantly. Recollection fades quickly, and it is sometimes hard to remember all the information you were unable to record on paper during the interview. Most importantly, dictate, or make a clear note of, what you advised and what it was decided to do next. These details can be surprisingly difficult to recall, especially if you have seen more than one new client in a day. You can create a standard form checklist if you find it helpful (see Appendix 2C).

Guard against your client accusing you later of saying something in the first interview which you cannot recall. His statement may be completely inaccurate, but it is hard to deny if you have no record of your advice. Clients who are distressed because of their personal circumstances do not always listen carefully or remember accurately. In the first interview, you have to impart a huge amount of technical information and explain a number of concepts which may be quite novel to your client. Many clients, even those whom you might have expected to understand, get completely muddled.

To avoid such misunderstandings write to your client, as soon as possible after the interview, setting out what the client told you and what you told the client. This has the double function of acting as an aide-mémoire for your client and a note on the file for you. It also enables you to pick up any points which may have been missed in the meeting. You should also confirm the position on costs, or public funding, of the case, and you should send your client details of the 'client care' provided by your firm, as set out in Chapter 13 of the *Guide to the Professional Conduct of Solicitors*.

Finally, do all the paperwork you possibly can before you close the file, including the public funding application. Have a break to get your concentration back and, as appropriate, discuss the client with your secretary, so that she has the benefit of your first impression and is better equipped to deal with any later contact.

SUMMARY

- Plan the interview carefully in advance.
- Consider the surroundings and the impression that you want to create.
- Keep a clear agenda in mind for the meeting.
- Be sure you know what your client wants.
- Give your client time to make a proper decision.
- Follow up the interview.
- Make a full note of your advice and all other important matters.

APPENDIX 2A

INSTRUCTIONS IN FAMILY PROCEEDINGS

DATE OF INSTRUCTIONS: MARRIAGE ☐   COHABITATION ☐

CLIENT   MRS ☐   MS ☐   MISS ☐   MR ☐

Full name:

Date of birth: Place of birth:

Address:

Address for correspondence if different from above:

Telephone numbers   Home: Work:

Occupation: Full time ☐

National Insurance number: Part time ☐   Number of hours worked per week ☐

Name and address of employers:

Health disabilities: 1

                                                2

SPOUSE/COHABITANT

Full name:

Date of birth: Place of birth:

Address: 3

Address for correspondence if different from above:

Telephone numbers   Home: Work:

Occupation: Full time ☐

National Insurance number: Part time ☐   Number of hours worked per week ☐

Name and address of employers:

Health disabilities:

Does s/he have a solicitor already?   Yes ☐   No ☐

Name and address:

Have proceedings been filed?   Yes ☐   No ☐

Details:

---

1   See Transaction Criteria 1.2(e). If appropriate, obtain signed authority to GP/Consultant for disclosure of medical details.

2   Cross-selling: is there a (potential) personal injury claim? Could damages be an issue?: *Wagstaff v Wagstaff* [1992] 1 FLR 333.

3   Check domicile/habitual residence if either address or place of marriage suggests foreign connection.

MARRIAGE

Date of marriage: [4] Place of marriage:

Status at marriage

Wife: single ☐ divorced ☐ widowed ☐   Husband: single ☐ divorced ☐ widowed ☐

Wife's surname at time of marriage:

Does client have official copy of marriage certificate?[5]

Religion   (Potentially) polygamous?[6]   YES ☐ NO ☐

MARRIAGE/COHABITATION

Date parties started living together:

Address where they last lived together:

Date of separation (if appropriate):

PREVIOUS PROCEEDINGS BETWEEN PARTIES   YES ☐ NO ☐

Nature:

Magistrates' court ☐

Injunction: county court ☐ magistrates' court ☐

Divorce ☐

Judicial separation ☐

CSA assessment ☐

Other ☐ Is any child adopted? YES ☐ NO ☐

Outcome:

CLS Funding: [7]

Did client have legal aid/CLS Funding?   YES ☐   NO ☐ NUMBER

Was there a full certificate?   YES ☐   NO ☐ [8]

Was there a Legal Help/Claim 10/Green Form?   YES ☐ NO ☐

Spouse/cohabitant's solicitors:

Have there been previous periods of separation?   YES ☐ NO ☐

Details:

---

4 If married under one year, advise appropriately.

5 If not, if client is to be Petitioner, arrange to obtain one or have client obtain one.

6 If marriage took place in country where polygamous marriage is permitted (even if there is no other wife), this must be dealt with in the petition. Rule 3.11, FPR 1991.

7 Obtain client's signature to letter requesting file from previous solicitors.

8 If appropriate, obtain authority for new Legal Help form and/or get client to sign request to the LSC for transfer of certificate to your firm.

CHILDREN OF THE FAMILY

If your client is the potential Petitioner, it may save time if you complete the Statement of Arrangements instead of this page at the first interview to save duplication. Otherwise, this page contains all the basic information which you need to gather at the outset, unless it is plain that there is an issue over the children which needs immediate attention. If this is the case, you will need to use an Attendance Note as well.

FULL NAME OF CHILD(REN)	DATE OF BIRTH	SCHOOL	State/Private

If there are any children born before the date of the marriage, confirm that
the husband is the father: YES ☐   NO ☐
If not, who is the father?
If not, why is a child 'child of the family'?

Does wife/husband have any other living children?

Who do the children of the family live with?

CHILDREN'S ACCOMMODATION

flat	☐	number of bedrooms	☐
house	☐	number of bathrooms	☐
maisonette	☐	kitchen	☐
other	☐ details:	number of living rooms	☐

Any other person sharing accommodation?

Present arrangements for looking after the children
Nanny's/minder's name:

CHILDREN'S HEALTH
Illnesses/chronic conditions:

GP/Hospital consultant:[9]

Welfare officer/social worker?

At risk register?

Present arrangements for contact:

Any problems over the issue of residence?[10]

---

9   If needed, obtain client's signed authority to GP/Consultant for disclosure of children's medical details.
10   If there are, you will need to consider the relevance of the factors or:
     ☐ religion
     ☐ ethnic origin and upbringing
     ☐ change of school
     ☐ accommodation offered by each party
     Use Attendance Note for recording further information if necessary.

FINANCE – CLIENT

If this form is being completed when divorce proceedings are anticipated, you may prefer to use Form E (ancillary relief) instead of the following three pages.

INCOME

EARNED INCOME

SALARY: GROSS £☐ per year ☐ month ☐ week ☐ NET £☐ per year ☐ month ☐ week ☐   [11]

OTHER EARNED INCOME £☐ details:

Bonuses: £☐ per year ☐ month ☐ week ☐

Overtime payments: £☐ per year ☐ month ☐ week ☐

BENEFITS IN KIND[12]

Car	YES ☐	NO ☐	Health insurance	YES ☐	NO ☐	
Petrol allowance	YES ☐	NO ☐	Pension scheme[13]	YES ☐	NO ☐	
Running expenses	YES ☐	NO ☐	Death in service benefit	YES ☐	NO ☐	
			Other	YES ☐	NO ☐	

UNEARNED INCOME — £ PER YEAR/MONTH/WEEK / £ PER YEAR/MONTH/WEEK

Housekeeping ☐   Pensions ☐
Maintenance: voluntary ☐ ☐   Share dividends ☐
cout order ☐   Rents ☐
CSA[14] ☐ ☐   Interest payments ☐
Trust ☐   Other ☐
Grant
Annuities ☐

STATE BENEFITS[15] — £ PER WEEK / £ PER WEEK

Child benefit ☐   Unemployment benefit ☐
(+ one parent benefit)   (Severe) disability allowance ☐
Income support ☐   Sickness benefit ☐
Family credit ☐   Disability working allowance ☐
  runs until when? ☐

CAPITAL[12] — DETAILS — £ — JT/SOLE

shares, premium bonds, building society, deposit accounts, national savings, insurance policies, jewellery, chattels, car(s), foreign assets, realty (other than matrimonial home), other?

DEBTS (Not secured) — DETAILS — £ — JT/SOLE

bank overdraft, credit cards, commercial personal loans, H.P., friends/family, other?

Give client outgoings questionnaire to take away and complete ☐ [16]

11 If part-time, what is the potential for an increase in the hours worked?
12 Fuller details can be obtained when a financial claim is made.
13 Obtain signed authority to pension trustee for disclosure of pension details.
14 Is there an application under the Child Support Act 1991? If not, would one be appropriate?
15 If party is unemployed, what is the potential for finding work?
16 See example at Appendix 7B.

FINANCE – SPOUSE/COHABITANT

(Position as far as is known to the client)

INCOME

EARNED INCOME

SALARY: GROSS £ [ ] per year ☐ month ☐ week ☐ NET £ [ ] per year ☐ month ☐ week ☐ [17]

OTHER EARNED INCOME £ [ ] details:

Bonuses: £ [ ] per year ☐ month ☐ week ☐

Overtime payments: £ [ ] per year ☐ month ☐ week ☐

BENEFITS IN KIND

Car	YES ☐	NO ☐	Health insurance	YES ☐	NO ☐
Petrol allowance	YES ☐	NO ☐	Pension scheme[13]	YES ☐	NO ☐
Running expenses	YES ☐	NO ☐	Death in service benefit	YES ☐	NO ☐
			Other	YES ☐	NO ☐

UNEARNED INCOME	£ PER YEAR/MONTH/WEEK		£ PER YEAR/MONTH/WEEK
Housekeeping	[ ]	Pensions	[ ]
Maintenance: voluntary ☐	[ ]	Share dividends	[ ]
cout order ☐		Rents	[ ]
CSA[18] ☐		Interest payments	[ ]
Trust	[ ]	Other	[ ]
Grant	[ ]		
Annuities	[ ]		

STATE BENEFITS[19]	£ PER WEEK		£ PER WEEK
Child benefit	[ ]	Unemployment benefit	[ ]
(+ one parent benefit)		(Severe) disability allowance	[ ]
Income support	[ ]	Sickness benefit	[ ]
Family credit	[ ]	Disability working allowance	[ ]
runs until when?	[ ]		

CAPITAL	DETAILS	£	JT/SOLE
shares		[ ]	
premium bonds		[ ]	
building society		[ ]	
deposit accounts		[ ]	
national savings		[ ]	
insurance policies		[ ]	
jewellery		[ ]	
chattels		[ ]	
car(s)		[ ]	
foreign assets		[ ]	
realty (other than matrimonial home)		[ ]	
other?		[ ]	

DEBTS (Not secured)	DETAILS	£	JT/SOLE
bank overdraft		[ ]	
credit cards		[ ]	
commercial personal loans		[ ]	
H.P.		[ ]	
Friends/family		[ ]	
other?		[ ]	

Give client outgoings questionnaire to take away and complete ☐ [16]

17 If part-time, what is the potential for an increase in the hours worked?
18 Is there an application under the Child Support Act 1991? If not, would one be appropriate?
19 If party is unemployed, what is the potential for finding work?

MATRIMONIAL HOME
OWNED PROPERTY

Owned by:[20]   Sole owner ☐   Joint tenants ☐   Tenants in common[21] ☐

Date of purchase:

Mortgagee:

Type of mortgage

Repayment   YES ☐   NO ☐

Endowment   YES ☐   NO ☐   Details of endowment policy(ies)
Other (specify)

Original amount lent: £

How balance provided:

Was the property purchased from the Council?   YES ☐   NO ☐

Was a discount given?   YES ☐   NO ☐

If so, what was the amount of the discount?   £ _____

When can the property be sold without the clawback? _____

Subsequent loans: date of loan
               lender
               amount
               purpose of loan[22]
               further endowments

Present value: £ _____   client's estimate ☐   (informal) valuation ☐
Current asking price: £ _____

Who pays mortgage?   Who pays endowment?

Amounts per month: £ _____   £ _____

Arrears?   £ _____

RENTED PROPERTY
Named tenant:

Landlord: name
             address

Deposit/Bond: YES ☐ NO ☐ Amount £ _____ Refundable? YES ☐ NO ☐ Amount £ _____
Rent: £ _____ per year ☐ month ☐ week ☐   Any arrears? £ _____

DOMESTIC FINANCES
(Outline who pays for what in the household budget, ie bills, food, children's needs)

---

20   Consider whether you need to register notice/caution of rights of occupation under the Matrimonial Homes Act 1983 ☐
21   Consider whether it is appropriate to serve a notice of severance either now or at a later stage in the proceedings ☐
22   If not for obvious joint purposes, did both parties consent to the loan and were both in occupation at the time when it was made? ☐

APPENDIX 2B

SUMMARY OF DIVORCE PROCEDURE

If the divorce or judicial separation is not defended the normal procedure is as follows:

PROCEEDINGS

LEGAL TERMS DEFINED

1. The PETITIONER's solicitors send the PETITION (and STATEMENT OF ARRANGEMENTS FOR CHILDREN if there are children) to the Court for filing.

The PETITIONER is the person who is applying for the divorce.

The PETITION is the legal document which sets out the reasons for the divorce or judicial separation.

STATEMENT OF ARRANGEMENTS FOR CHILDREN is a form which tells the Court about the children's living arrangements. If possible, both husband and wife should sign this in advance.

2. The Court sends the copy Petition and the ACKNOWLEDGEMENT OF SERVICE to the RESPONDENT (and CO-RESPONDENT).

ACKNOWLEDGEMENT OF SERVICE is the official form to complete and sign to show that the Respondent has received the Petition, and whether s/he intends to defend it or not.

RESPONDENT is the person who is being divorced.

CO-RESPONDENT in cases of adultery is the named person with whom the adultery was committed.

3. The Respondent (and Co-respondent) complete answers to the questions on the acknowledgement of service and send it back to the Court.

4. The Court send photocopy of the acknowledgement of service to the Petitioner's solicitors.

5. The Petitioner's solicitors prepare the AFFIDAVIT IN SUPPORT OF THE PETITION for the Petitioner to swear.

AFFIDAVIT IN SUPPORT OF THE PETITION is a written statement under oath telling the Court that the contents of the Petition are true and saying that the Petitioner wants to proceed with the divorce.

6. The Petitioner's solicitors send the sworn Affidavit to the Court together with REQUEST FOR DIRECTIONS FOR TRIAL.

REQUEST FOR DIRECTIONS FOR TRIAL is a form asking the Court to fix a date for Decree Nisi.

7. The Court fixes the date and time of the pronouncement of DECREE NISI (or Judicial Separation) and, if there are children, it also considers the arrangements for the children which have been set out by the husband and wife. If the Judge is satisfied s/he will give a certificate stating this and no appointment at court will be required. (In some cases the Judge may want parents to provide further information about the children.) The Court sends out the notice of the time and date of Decree Nisi to both Petitioner and Respondent or to their solicitors.

DECREE NISI is the first decree of divorce. It is a provisional decree and does not dissolve the marriage finally.

8. Decree Nisi is pronounced. Generally, no attendance is necessary.

9. Six weeks and one day after Decree Nisi the Petitioner can apply for DECREE ABSOLUTE to be made, by sending a form to the Court (provided, if there are children, that the Judge is satisfied with the arrangements for them).

DECREE ABSOLUTE is the final decree of divorce. Once it is made the marriage is at an end and both parties may remarry if they wish to do so. The Decree Absolute is not made by the Court unless one party requests it. There are sometimes good reasons for delaying the application which you should discuss with your solicitor.

If the Petitioner delays applying for more than three months after this date then the Respondent can apply, by requesting the Court to fix an appointment to consider the matter. The Petitioner can object to this.

APPENDIX 2C

ACTION PLAN

CLIENT NAME: _____   DATE: _____

☐ PETITIONER   ☐ RESPONDENT   ☐ COHABITEE APPLICANT   ☐ RESPONDENT
☐ Adultery   ☐ Property claim
☐ Behaviour
☐ Desertion
☐ Separation 2 years ☐
          5 years ☐   ☐ Violence/Injunction   ☐ Violence/Injunction
                              ☐ Residence   ☐ Residence
                              ☐ Contact   ☐ Contact
                              ☐ Maintenance   ☐ Paternity issue   ☐ Maintenance
☐ Ancillary relief   ☐ Lump sum for child(ren)

WHAT DOES CLIENT WANT TO ACHIEVE?

ADVISED ON: CLIENT GIVEN:
☐ Divorce and matrimonial proceedings generally   ☐ Information about divorce proceedings[1]
☐ Financial principles: property rights   ☐ Client care letter
☐ Welfare benefits   ☐ CLS forms to complete
☐ Tax   ☐ Information about mediation services
☐ Injunction law and procedure   ☐ Outgoings questionnaire[2]
☐ Time scale   ☐ Form E to complete
☐ Will   ☐ Other?
☐ Other?

INITIAL ACTION TO BE TAKEN:
☐ Letter to other party/solicitors
☐ Copy to client
☐ Draft [_____] to client
☐ Proceedings for [_____] to be filed
☐ Take emergency action
☐ Apply for (emergency) CLS funding
☐ Wait for further instructions
☐ (Client to) obtain marriage certificate/other documents:
☐ Other:

COSTS
FUNDED CLIENT:
☐ Informed about Green Form/Legal Help
☐ Informed about Approved Family Help/Legal Representation
☐ Informed about Statutory Charge
☐ Informed about potential personal liability for costs if certificate revoked
☐ Estimate of costs given, how much? £ [_____]
PRIVATE CLIENT:
☐ Payment on account requested: how much? £ [_____]
☐ If instalments, how much? £ [_____] how often? [_____]
☐ Standing order?
☐ Estimate of costs given, how much? £ [_____]

1   For example of a summary of divorce procedure, see Appendix 2B.
2   See example at Appendix 7B.

Chapter 3

THE DIFFICULT CLIENT

Lawyers say that family lawyers get sacked by their clients more often than their colleagues in other fields of the law. This may or may not be true, but it underlines the different nature of the solicitor/client relationship in family law, which is susceptible to great tensions and upsets.

The purpose of this chapter is to explore the things that can go wrong in your relationship with your client and to help you avoid some of the obvious pitfalls.

DIFFICULT PEOPLE

Some clients are simply difficult people and there is little you can do to change their basic nature. It may be that it forms part of the reason for the marriage breakdown. More often your client may be difficult because she is frightened and distressed by what is happening in her life. Try to assume that this is the case for all your clients (although you may be driven to the first conclusion eventually). If you can bear her difficulties in mind when you deal with her, it will help you to summon up your reserves of patience and tolerance; these may help you to comfort her and make her feel better.

CLIENTS WHO DO NOT WANT YOU TO BE A SOLICITOR

One of the chief sources of difficulty with clients springs from their expectation that you can fulfil a role which is additional to that of legal adviser. This often arises from a failure on their part to grasp your real role in the divorce. It is not easy to define that role, and is often easier to say what you are not, but this too is complicated because you do wear a number of different hats.

For example, you are not a counsellor to your client; yet sometimes your contact with her leads you into that role. The danger comes when your client wants you to assume that role permanently. Even if you are a trained counsellor, you will be aware that you cannot combine the two roles without causing problems for both you and your client.

It is sometimes difficult to know when this problem has arisen. You may have nothing more to guide you than a vague feeling of unease about some of the things your client says when you are talking to her. The danger signs seem to be when she becomes frustrated with you when you try to take instructions. She may say something like 'You're the solicitor. I want you to ...'; very often fulfilling her request would involve abandoning your function as a solicitor. I have found that it helps if you identify what it is you think the client wants you to be, put this to your client and explain that you do not think that it is part of your function. Sometimes, this clears matters up between you. Unfortunately, a client may object to your suggestion and try to resist your attempt to clarify your role.

However, it will still help you to deal with the problem if you have defined it. If the client goes on behaving in this way, you may have to renew the conversation and try to explain the difficulties it causes for you.

I try, in this chapter, to identify some of the roles into which clients try to push you. With all of them, part of your art as a solicitor is that you need to take certain aspects from them, but you have to be careful not to take on these roles completely or you may lose your professional detachment and ability to be flexible.

The friend

You need to be friendly to your clients certainly, and it may end up at the end of the case that you are friends, but you cannot afford to fall into this role while you are acting as your client's legal adviser. If this seems odd, think about what it would be like to act in a divorce for one of your own friends. The relationship would need to be extraordinary for it not to end in disaster. This is because friendship generally demands a degree of partisanship which sits uneasily with professional detachment.

Unfortunately, clients who are feeling vulnerable after their marriage break-down may well interpret your pleasant manner as an overture of real friendship and be desperate to push you in that direction. If this starts to happen, you may need to be cooler and more remote, without being harsh, to prevent it. Generally make it your practice to address your client formally as 'Mrs Brown' or 'Mrs Smith', etc, even if your client uses your first name.

The counsellor

As I have already observed, trying to be your client's counsellor can be a dangerous role because part of your function does involve you in being a counsellor from time to time. But counselling, in its technical professional sense, approaches therapy in its techniques, and the trouble with mixing it with family law is that it demands more time than your client can afford or than public funding will pay for.

You may also need to be much more directional than a therapist should be. The technique of counselling involves, in part, getting the client to come to her own decisions and solutions by a process of working through her feelings while you listen and reflect her thoughts back to her. You know that being a solicitor is not always like that; you may have to ask your client to make a quick, clear decision between two courses of action, and you may have to recommend one course of action because of the consequences that you, as a lawyer, foresee.

If your client starts to use you as a counsellor, you can point this out to her and suggest that she has some counselling from an agency that you can recommend (see Chapter 4).

Father / authority figures

Some clients want you to make all the decisions for them. Some want you to take all the responsibility for what happens. This gives them a good excuse to say 'It's not my fault, it's my solicitor's'. Very often such a client will say something like 'Well you're the solicitor; it's your job to advise me', in response to a letter in which you have set out possible alternatives. They do not want you to advise, they want you to make choices for them, and you may have to be quite tough in your response. Other clients have never got in the habit of taking any decisions for themselves. The whole history of their marriage has been one of domination by the other party. In these cases, you need to help your client by encouraging her to experience the heady (and alarming) joys of making her own decisions at last. You may need to take things gently but, if you do not do this and make the decisions for her, you perpetuate the pattern of her marriage. She will have a life after divorce, and she has to get ready to lead that life without your tender ministrations. Otherwise, you are stuck with the problem of the former client who keeps ringing you long after your retainer is ended.

Knights on white chargers

Some clients do not really want a legal adviser, they want an uncritical champion of their cause. They are upset if you point out the possible weaknesses of their case. These clients will take advice only if it is what they want to hear, and are liable to shop around until they find someone unscrupulous enough to give it to them. Such an attitude needs to be confronted. You need to explain that this is not your role. Your role is to give your client the best possible advice about how to achieve what they want; that includes giving a realistic appraisal of how realistic that goal is and, if it is not realistic, to suggest viable alternatives. If this does not work you are probably wasting your time trying to act for such a client. Sooner or later, your instructions will be withdrawn.

Hired guns

This is slightly different from the knightly role. Some clients want you to be a particular sort of aggressive frightener to their spouse. This may sit comfortably with your view of who you are, but it does not go with the SFLA approach which, I am bound to say, is best for the client and you in the long run. If you already espouse the SFLA ideal, you will have to explain to your client that you cannot readily take on the gun-slinger role and it will not do your client much good if you do (see 'Aggressive clients' below).

RUDE CLIENTS

Some clients are habitually rude. This is difficult to deal with because it is unpleasant and can provoke you to be rude in return. If this happens, your client may blame you. Whoever is to blame, this will reflect badly on you because you will have betrayed your own professional standards and put yourself at a further disadvantage in dealing with the client.

Sometimes you are well aware that your client's rudeness stems from the predicament which brings her to see you, and she is taking it out on you because you are an easy target. Part of your function as a matrimonial solicitor is to act as an emotional buffer between spouses. Rudeness is something you have to be able to absorb, but it does no harm to point out, firmly but gently, and with as much humour as you can muster, that there is no point in the client taking it out on you because you are supposed to be looking after her. However, it is unproductive to make comments such as 'I am on your side', which reinforce the image of two diametrically opposed parties. It may be more effective to say something like 'Look, I know that you are very upset, but I do find it very hard when you take it out on me when I am trying to do my best for you', rather than trying to be tough in your response which generally gets you into an argument or, worse, the defence/attack spiral.

In another context, I once had to deal with someone who was intent on picking a fight with me when I was holding a sleeping baby in my arms. It taught me an invaluable lesson. I was determined not to wake the baby up and so spoke very quietly throughout the confrontation. I found that it is almost impossible for the other person to continue to work the argument up when you respond in this way. The quieter you speak, the better you can make your points. And, if you make a conscious effort to stay physically relaxed (as I had to, or wake the sleeping infant), this helps you also to control your response.

It is always a good idea to try the nice approach first to see whether this will calm the client down, but some clients may be immune to this. It may get to the point where you have to tell them that you are not prepared to continue to act unless they improve their behaviour. For instance, you may find it unacceptable when a client habitually uses offensive language; if you point this out, many clients will apologise and try to moderate their speech.

AGGRESSIVE CLIENTS

Often rudeness and aggression go together, but there is also a special category of aggressive client. I have in mind the client who finds it very difficult to express his feelings about what has happened and so tends to take an aggressive and abrupt stance about the things you need to discuss. You may find that such clients are very reticent about a number of issues that you regard as critical. They may see litigation as the solution to every problem and feel that the only way to proceed is to coerce the other party by any means available. You can find yourself being treated as one of those means.

If you do not feel that this is the right approach, you must take a firm position to defend your professional standards. You are not there to be used as a tool by your client, even though you are acting on his instructions. If your client wants you to do something which you regard as wrong you have to say why and stick to your guns. This is not always easy, particularly in the case of the client who is used to having his own way or who is an 'important' client of the firm. You may have to invoke the help of a senior colleague with whom you can discuss your difficulties, who can, if necessary, be asked to take the matter up with the client.

OBSESSIVE, LOQUACIOUS AND OVER-EMOTIONAL CLIENTS

Some clients may have one or all of these characteristics, and I have lumped them together because I think that they create similar problems for the legal adviser. They tend to be so intent on their agenda that it can be very difficult to conduct any sort of meeting with them. Here the best technique is to be rather more heavy-handed with your agenda. There are clients for whom I would consider writing down a list of topics, either in a letter before a meeting or at the beginning of the meeting. I would stress that I am doing this so as to save them costs, and I would draw them back to the agenda if they start to stray. It is important for these clients to focus on what the real legal issues are and make them aware that other matters, though important to them in other aspects of their life, are not what your job is about.

SEXIST AND RACIST CLIENTS

I remember being pretty startled when one of my 'respectable' middle class 'lady' clients said, when I raised the question of the barrister whom we needed to instruct, 'I don't care who you choose so long as he isn't black'. There are two neat examples of prejudice in there, neither of which I felt inclined to pander to. In such cases you can turn to the *Rules of Professional Conduct* for help. If your client persists in such a view you may decline to act. Indeed, you are obliged to decline if your client insists that you follow her instructions. It may be easier to explain your difficulty by using the Rules as an excuse, rather than your own moral code. I say this not because I think that you should not stand up for your principles, but, by doing so, you make the argument seem too personal – as though you are setting yourself up as a judge of your client's character. You may in fact be doing this privately, but it may make your relationship very difficult if you voice this to the client.

ANALYSING THE PROBLEM

Your feelings obviously have a lot to do with whether you will find one client more difficult than others. I have dealt with these in the introduction. If you have a difficult relationship with a client you will need to consider what part your feelings play and what control you can exercise over them. But often there is more to be learned from the relationship than that. It is tempting to dismiss a difficult client because thinking about it is painful for you, but, if you try to analyse the situation, you may well learn from it and be able to bring what you have learned to other relationships with clients, thus becoming better at what you do.

Remember, it is not always the client's fault. If you are aware that a problem has arisen wholly or partly because of your own attitude, try to see what you can do to change it, and to become more amenable to your client. If the difficulty is because of your client's attitude, try to work out its cause. Sometimes, 'To understand all is to forgive all'. Understanding may help you to be more tolerant, which may relax your client and improve the solicitor/client relationship.

It may help if you are frank with your client and confess that you perceive a problem in your relationship with her. This can lead to a discussion about how you can get back on a better footing with each other, although this sometimes backfires. I once confessed to a client that I sometimes found it difficult to know what she wanted. She invited me out to lunch, which was very amicable, and sacked me the following day.

Do not be afraid to apologise if a client complains. Explain, if you can, why you have said or done something. If you have made a mistake, own up to it and apologise. Talk through the difficulty. Clients are quick to detect a cover-up and are not comforted by it.

CLIENTS WITH MENTAL PROBLEMS

As a matrimonial lawyer, you will encounter a wide spectrum of odd behaviour. You will meet families who are 'merely' dysfunctional, clients who are more or less autistic, or clients with peculiar neuroses or phobias.

Some clients, however, may be truly mentally ill, although this is not always apparent when you first take them on. If there is a long history of mental illness, this may be the reason why the marriage has broken down. If it becomes apparent to you that your client is not capable of giving you proper instructions and you believe that she may be suffering from some disability, you need to consider whether she should have a 'litigation friend' appointed for her.

If so, the first stage is to get a doctor's opinion, but this can be difficult because in order to do so you need the consent of the client. Some clients may agree to your suggestion to consult their doctor, others may become very angry at the suggestion that they are 'mad' and you will need to use your powers of persuasion to obtain the necessary authority. In some cases you may have to tell your client that you cannot continue to act under the public funding application unless you are satisfied as to the state of their health.

You can consult the Official Solicitor's Department and find out what it recommends. I have always found the Department very helpful.

LOSING THE CLIENT

Despite all your efforts (and sometimes because of them), your client may decide to go elsewhere. If she does, this is probably for the best. If she has been difficult you have probably been devoting a disproportionate amount of time to worrying about the case.

Be gracious about it. If papers are called for, send them on as quickly as possible. If you need to render a bill, do it courteously and quickly. If the client is publicly funded, and it is appropriate, write to the CLS to confirm your consent to the transfer of papers immediately, obtain an undertaking to preserve your lien for costs, arrange for the assessment of your costs and pass the file over straightaway, rather than wait to hear from the CLS telling you to do so. If you do not feel that it is appropriate for your client to change, again, respond to the CLS swiftly.

COMPLAINTS TO THE OFFICE FOR THE SUPERVISION OF SOLICITORS (OSS)

One day someone is going to complain about you, however good you are. It can be upsetting and infuriating if you know that the complaint is unjustified, but you will not make the position any better by delaying your response, even if the OSS has taken its time to write to you.

Clearly, you need to deal with any complaint according to the procedure laid down in your office. Write as full an explanation as possible in an effort to deal with the complaint in one letter, rather than entering into lengthy correspondence which makes it look as if an explanation is being dragged out of you. Remember that the OSS will send a copy of your letter to the client. Do not be afraid to admit to a mistake if you made one. If you are worried that such an admission might be construed as an admission of negligence, you should make sure that it has first been cleared by the person in the firm who has responsibility for professional insurance and, if necessary, by the insurers themselves.

SHARE YOUR PROBLEM

In all aspects of your professional life your colleagues are generally the best source of help and advice, and this is particularly so when you are faced with a difficult client. Do not bottle up the trouble, even if you feel shy about confessing the difficulty you are having. Your colleagues can help in all kinds of ways, from suggesting useful strategies you might employ, to arranging to relieve you of the client. Sometimes, the very act of talking about the problem helps you to arrive at your own solution, or strengthens you to deal with the situation the next time it arises. Similarly, dictating a long note analysing the difficulties can help you to find a way through them.

SUMMARY

- Do not allow yourself to be forced into roles which are not compatible with your professional task.
- Work out why the client is being rude to you.
- Maintain your professional standards.
- Be alert for mentally ill clients.
- If your client sacks you, be gracious about it.
- If you are the subject of a complaint, act promptly and sensibly.
- Share your problems.

Chapter 4

USING OUTSIDE AGENCIES

Your resources as a lawyer are finite. Some clients clearly have needs which cannot be met by you as their legal adviser but you may want to offer help. However, you cannot do everything for your client and you have to know when to stop. You cannot wear too many hats without confusing your role and making your position, and eventually that of your client, more difficult. The constraints of costs, particularly in publicly funded cases, mean that you cannot depart too far from the role of giving legal advice. None of this means that you have to abandon your client and leave her resourceless.

TYPES OF AGENCIES AVAILABLE

There are two principal categories of agency. The first is the mediation agency, which provides an alternative to the service you give. The second comprises the many different advice and aid agencies which tackle areas outside your immediate expertise, such as housing agencies or single-parent groups.

MEDIATION

Background

When I wrote the first edition of this book I stated that 'the proper use of conciliation/mediation is a topic of great controversy and debate among family lawyers'. Since then mediation ('conciliation' seems to have been almost dropped as a term) has become more common. There are well-established mediation services. Mediation has been built into the process of obtaining public funding. It has government approval, even if it is still not adequately funded, and a good deal of research has taken place about its effect on divorcing couples, and the costs.

Mediation has generally been seen as a 'good thing', if only because of its emphasis on trying to get the couple to be civilised towards each other. It was promoted still further at around the time the Family Law Act 1996 was being debated and enacted. At that point mediation seemed to offer an expedient way of reducing costs and therefore the legal aid (as it then was) cost to the state. Some more cynical lawyers also concluded that there was the motive of reducing the time the courts had to spend dealing with family law disputes.

Since then it has become apparent that mediation is not the panacea politicians might have hoped. Only a minority (15%–25%) of the cases that are referred as part of the CLS funding process are assessed as being suitable for mediation. Also, recent studies have shown that it is not necessarily cheaper. Mediation services, like any professional service dealing with people's personal problems, need trained, professional people and suitable premises, and this needs adequate and reliable funding if clients are to be satisfied with the level of service they get.

Referring clients to mediation

There seem to be two main stumbling blocks in referring clients to a mediation service.

The first is that you have to be fairly sure that the service will offer them something different to the service you can offer and that it is something they need. If you have not seen a mediation in action or had much to do with mediation it may be hard for you to accept that sometimes a different approach may work.

If you do observe mediations in action your first reaction as a solicitor may be impatience. A lot of time may be spent going over issues that you feel are not relevant, or where you feel that a single letter from you or an order from the court would slice through the problem more efficiently. Mediation is not just about reaching an agreement; it is also a process intended to allow the couple to reach that agreement internally, as a matter of choice and will, rather than having to submit to something imposed on them. Sometimes we may be inclined to treat our clients as children who do not know what is good for them, so we impose the solution on them. We do this for the best of motives, as most parents would. Sometimes our clients will be truly grateful for this, because we have relieved them of an oppressive responsibility. But they are not children; they are adults at a vulnerable time of their lives.

So bottle the impatience and talk to the mediators about the way they go about the process and why they think it has value. There are an increasing number of solicitor mediators, and you may find it helpful to discuss your concerns with them. This may enable you to spot the client for whom mediation may be truly helpful. If you are able to, recommend to your client that she explores the possibility of mediation with an open mind. One of the main problems mediation services face at the initial appointment is that the solicitor has already denigrated the idea of mediation to the client so that she is prejudiced against it.

The second problem in making a referral is that you are sending work (and fees) away from your office. In these circumstances, how can you be wholehearted about the idea? You may have to toe the line of your firm's policy on this. My view is that the client who is suitable for mediation and is recommended to it by you will come back for advice on the settlement and will recommend you to friends because you will be viewed as having acted fairly and sensibly. In this way your professional reputation will be enhanced.

Points to bear in mind in considering a referral

In suggesting to a client that he should make use of a mediation agency you are acknowledging the limitations of the process in which you are involved. This is more difficult than admitting to the limits of your advice-giving powers which you must face when referring clients to the second category of agencies I have mentioned. It is important, as I suggest later in this chapter, that you do not give the impression that you just want the client off your hands.

It is generally easier to come to the conclusion that mediation might help in matters concerning children. Very often the limitations of Legal Help leave you with little scope for any other suggestion. Children's issues are more susceptible to mediation. As a moral issue, it is easier for parents to agree that children should not be the subject of litigation, and they more readily appreciate that they need to find a way of continuing to operate as parents even though they are no longer spouses. Often, it will be plain to you that the real problem is a failure to communicate rather than a real issue of principle. Even your client may be able to analyse the problem in this way. Mediation is clearly worth trying in such circumstances.

There are greater difficulties when financial issues need to be resolved. The technical problem for lawyers relates to disclosure; even the best-regulated agencies cannot ensure that both parties disclose their assets fully, and without such a safeguard clients can be vulnerable. However, many mediation services now use a form for disclosure similar to Form E. It is possible to argue that the process of disclosure is overdone in most cases and that, where people's finances are straightforward, the intervention of a solicitor is not necessary. In such cases, mediation may offer a cheaper and more harmonious way of dealing with the distribution of assets.

The motivation of some of the people who choose to go to mediation is the real problem. There is a broad group of people who are reasonably amicable about their divorces and who are confident both in their own ability to negotiate and in the honesty of their spouses. For these people, mediation can be an excellent way of sorting things out, although they would probably arrive at similar solutions and remain amicable if they used solicitors. My real worry is the people who choose mediation because they think that in this way they will be able to exploit the absence of solicitors to their personal advantage.

There are some clients who insist on going to mediation, and use the process for their own ends, dragging out the resolution of the matter by refusing to give full and frank disclosure and by perpetuating the exercise of emotional and fiscal power which has characterised their married lives. Their spouses often agree at first to mediation because they have acceded to the other's wishes throughout the marriage.

Only rarely will the process of mediation be effective in such cases. It is essentially a voluntary procedure, so people come to it on their own terms. Unless they genuinely accept the ethos of the process, mediation cannot work.

The balance of power in marriages

One of the problems in resolving the difficulties of any broken marriage is redressing the balance of power. Generally, husbands are more powerful because they have the financial edge. They are often psychologically more powerful because they have been used to having their own way in the marriage. Wives are seldom as assertive, either financially or emotionally. A surprising number of women know little of their husband's financial affairs and lack confidence when talking about pensions or investments. Often, the only 'bargaining counter' which they have is the children, but it is quite common for a wife consulting you to feel deeply insecure about her position as a mother and for her to be sure that she will lose the children if she puts a foot wrong. One of my colleagues sagely observed that at the beginning of a case male clients tend to be sure that they will win and female clients tend to feel that they will lose.

Part of your role as a solicitor is to redress that balance of power. You must explain to your female client that she is not as weak as she imagines, or has been led to imagine; that she has legal rights; that the court will protect her; that the children are unlikely to be taken away, and that she can get public funding. The fact that you take her seriously can give her confidence. On the other hand, with a male client, you may have to explain that he is not able to act as freely as he may have done during his marriage; that he cannot conceal his assets; that he has to give his wife a fair share; and that trying to bully her is likely to be counter-productive.

One of the limitations of mediation is that it does not always seem to have the means to deal effectively with the imbalance between spouses. Mediators may not be as tough with their clients as you can be with yours. It is difficult to say whether this is because of the nature of the process or the approach of the people who work as mediators.

The better balance of power in matters involving children may be one of the reasons why mediation works better for these cases. A woman may often feel more confident, partly because her own importance as their mother is not in doubt and partly because she is not ashamed to make a stand for them. This is something which society approves and recognises – the cliché of the tigress protecting her whelps – but a woman fighting for money attracts all sorts of opprobrious terms such as 'gold-digger' or 'alimony drone'.

Advantages of mediation

It is not my intention to put you off the idea of mediation, but I think it is as well to be aware of the potential pitfalls. In the right circumstances, mediation is enormously helpful, and your clients will be pleased that you referred them, but there are cases where you may have to be cautious and select the agency very carefully.

At best, mediation helps clients to take control of their lives in a positive way. It often restores communication between spouses, and in some cases makes it better than it has been for a long time. It is often cheaper than using solicitors and may well be more efficient, for instance in dealing with the arrangements for access. Clients often return to you in a more positive frame of mind to deal with those matters within your expertise.

HOW TO REFER TO OTHER AGENCIES

Clients can naturally be fairly resistant to being referred to someone else. They have got used to you, they like the way that you handle things, they may feel that at last there is someone who really understands them and now you are packing them off to someone new. It is easy for them to feel rejected, particularly if their self-esteem is low. You must, therefore, be careful in the way in which you put the idea to the client. If your client is applying for public funding, it can be a help because you have probably already explained to your client the limitations which this imposes, but in private cases it is not an appropriate approach.

You need to be ready with an explanation of the limitations of your job as a lawyer; to explain to your client that he has needs which you are not trained to fulfil, that you will, of course, try your best as his legal adviser, but that he also needs extra help from someone else. Everyone likes to feel special and important, and it is this that you need to emphasise to your client. It is very helpful to know the names of the people you are sending him to. If you can ring them in the company of your client and give them some of the background, your client will know that you are treating him as an individual.

It is also important to point out that you are not abandoning him. You want to know what happens, and you would like him to report back to you. If he does not feel that the agency is being helpful, you would like to know. This is not merely cosmetic. You really do need to monitor what happens and find out whether it is worth continuing to refer your clients to a particular agency.

CLIENT RESISTANCE

Mediation is now well known, and clients will understand that mediators are working for them. There may be other problems if you want to refer clients to agencies like Family Welfare. It is difficult to refer clients to whom the idea of anyone outside the family intervening is alien and frightening. They fear social workers because of the stigma their involvement carries with them, and because of a latent terror that their children might be taken away. They associate therapy with madness. You need to spend a fair amount of time educating such clients about what such agencies really offer. Avoid talking about the staff as social workers, emphasise that the agency is independent, point out that any referral to the agency is a voluntary matter for your client, and stress that information is treated as confidential. Give a potted explanation of the theory behind the process and make it clear that family therapy does not imply that there is something wrong with the family.

Another type of client whom it is difficult to refer tends to be at the other end of the spectrum, ie too sophisticated. Such clients are likely to be professional people, often working in a similar field to the agency. You will have little difficulty explaining to them that mediation is valuable, but you may find that they are frustrated by the agency you use. They can see through the techniques which are being used on them and may resent the process. They may feel that they are better educated and more professional in their approach than the staff of the agency and feel reluctant to participate. You cannot win in such cases. You can warn them in advance that the process may require an effort of will on their part and they may find that some of it appears to be simplistic and childish. You can try to direct them to agencies which you know are run in a more sophisticated way. When you have such clients and you feel that mediation is needed, it may be better to try to achieve this by a round table meeting with both clients and both solicitors.

If your client is very resistant, there is little you can do. You can abandon the subject if it looks like becoming a difficulty between you, but keep it in mind to return to at a later stage if circumstances allow. You have to take a conscious decision about the extent to which you are going to let your client push you into a role for which you think the agency would be better suited. If you feel that you cannot act effectively in that role then you have to make this clear to your client and stand firm.

INVOLVING THE OTHER PARTY'S ADVISERS

If you feel that mediation would help your client you are not likely to be successful in a referral unless the adviser acting for the other spouse also backs the referral. A telephone call to put him in the picture and see whether you can both recommend mediation would probably be the best approach.

You may, of course, find the other lawyer resistant to the suggestion, if only on the 'taking bread out my mouth' argument. You cannot threaten or coerce co-operation. All you can do is point out what you think the advantages might be.

Sometimes your client will feel that she can approach her husband directly and discuss it between them, and this may be the best way. You, of course, cannot approach him directly unless he is acting in person.

COMPILING A LIST OF AGENCIES

It will help you if you get together a list of agencies to which you can refer your clients. You will inevitably create such a list in time, but you can speed up the process by making a conscious effort to find out what is available in your local area and by making preliminary inquiries of the organisations and individuals concerned.

At the back of this book there is a list of relevant national organisations. You also need to find out about local services. The following list of local offices and organisations is a useful starting point for your research:

- local authority social services department;
- local authority housing department;
- local housing associations;
- advice agencies, on housing, debt, etc;
- local churches, which have associated help agencies, eg the Church of England employs social workers of its own in the local boards of social responsibility. Some local churches run marriage counselling, or unemployment counselling;
- health visitors – every mother with a baby has one assigned, via the local child health clinic. These can be a great source of support and practical advice, especially to young mothers;
- neighbourhood centres;
- mediation services;
- agencies catering for particular ethnic groups.

Local authorities may produce directories of these agencies, or the local library may keep their brochures and will let you have them. However, you may have to ask around among your colleagues and local contacts.

Once you have found a useful agency it helps if you can find out the name of one or two members of staff so that you can get to know them, if only on the phone. This can improve client referrals. You can also find out whether there is a preferred method of referral; would they prefer you to ring or write to them or would they prefer to speak to your client direct?

As well as providing a better service to your client, making referrals to other agencies has advantages to you in the marketing field. These are dealt with at greater length in Chapter 14. You can also acquire skills and information from such agencies which enhance your professional capacity.

SUMMARY

- Using outside agencies judiciously enhances your ability to look after your clients.
- Mediation can be enormously helpful, but has its pitfalls.
- Build up a list of useful agencies.
- Build up a network of personal contacts.

Chapter 5

COMMUNICATING AND PAPERWORK

Before I deal with specific aspects of cases, it is worthwhile considering the way lawyers communicate and prepare paperwork.

LANGUAGE

It is depressing to learn that lawyers are traditionally considered to be poor communicators given that words are the tools of our trade. It is only recently that communicating with clients has been acknowledged as an important part of training for lawyers.

It is particularly important in the field of family law that you communicate properly with your client. As a rule, family law clients have had little or no contact with a lawyer before they come to see you. They may be upset, which will mean that they are not able to listen carefully, and you need to build a personal relationship with them based on respect and trust as quickly as you can. To achieve this, your clients need to understand what is happening at each stage of the proceedings.

Some clients' inability to understand verbal or written information may come as a shock to you. Some of your clients may not even be able to read. Do not assume either that well-educated clients will necessarily understand everything you write or say to them without further explanation. Often your client will be so upset and under such stress that he will find it difficult to comprehend what may seem to you to be the simplest part of the procedure.

I was once completely disconcerted by the following dialogue with a client of mine who was a professional woman and a graduate.

Me: And then I will make an application for financial relief for you.
Client: What does that mean?
Me: We will ask the court to make all the sorts of financial orders that they can ... maintenance ... lump sum orders ... a transfer of property.
Client: What do you mean make an application?
Me: Well ..., I lodge the papers asking for the order at the court.
Client: What does that mean?

Me. I send the papers to the court and they put them on your file which is the official notification to the court that you want to pursue your claims.
Client. What does that mean?

I gave up fairly soon after that and suggested that I wrote it down for her and that she got the *Which? Guide to Divorce* out of the library. My mistake was to assume that the technical terms were self-evident and she would have some notion of the mechanics of the process.

KEEP IT SIMPLE

You may be worried that if you write simply your client will think that she is not getting a 'proper' lawyer, because her expectation will be that you will use a stream of long words. But this is not the case in my experience. Clients may expect that you will be difficult to understand, but they will be very pleased to find that this is not the case and may even express their relief and pleasure at finding out that you are human after all.

Try to purge your remarks and letters of too much technical jargon. You cannot do it completely without becoming woolly in the way you describe things, but you can try to get rid of such terms as 'ancillary relief', or remember to explain it when you use it frequently so your client understands. I have already suggested that it is helpful to give your client a sheet which explains the divorce procedure and defines the technical terms.

Do not slip into the use of legal phrases which will not convey much to your client. Terms like 'inter alia', 'inst.', 'ult.', can be baffling. Archaic phrases such as 'hereinbefore' and 'the same' should also be avoided. This applies to letters to other practitioners as much as to clients. It might help to develop a style which suits all your correspondence. Your letters may need to be copied for other people, so they need to be comprehensible all round.

KEEP IT SHORT

Make sure that your letters are easy to read. Try to keep paragraphs short and subordinate clauses to a minimum. Use a clear, large typeface which is well spaced out. Where there are a number of issues you need your client or the other lawyer to deal with, consider writing separate letters about each one.

KEEP IT CLEAR

If you are making a number of points in a letter and you want to draw attention to each of them, put them in separate paragraphs and number them so that they act as a checklist.

If you are sending your client a number of documents which you want her to read, sign and send back to you, number each document and list them in your letter (for instance with a detachable label) numbered accordingly to make it as clear as possible which is which, and explain what you want your client to do with each one.

Read your letters, trying to see how they would sound if you knew nothing about the law. Beware of ambiguity. A colleague of mine once wrote to a client 'Please sign the enclosed document where I have indicated your initials in pencil'. So the client signed the document in pencil! I encountered a similar reaction from clients to whom I wrote sending an affidavit in support of the petition. My standard letter used to end 'Once you have sworn it please return it to me . . .', and they would come into the office and insist on seeing me just to hand the document over. It took me a long time to realise that the reason they were not posting it, as I had assumed they would, was the way I had phrased the letter. I changed it to read 'Once you have sworn it please send it back to me', and the number of people who brought it in personally dropped dramatically.

FORMAL DOCUMENTS

When you are drafting a sworn statement or particulars try to keep to your client's way of expressing herself as far as possible. You may have to iron out the grammar at some points, and possibly take out slang which the judge might not understand (or might make a show of not understanding), but otherwise try to keep close to her vocabulary and style.

This is important because you are going to give the document to your client and expect her, once she has checked the contents, to swear to the truth of it. Many clients take the sanguine view that if you, as the lawyer, have drafted it, it must be true! If you have written it in language your client cannot understand she can easily get confused and, if a point like this is seized on when your client is giving evidence, she can be made to look like a liar when the truth is that she has simply gone along with what you wrote.

When you are drafting something which does not have to be in a prescribed form try to write it in standard English, not legalese. For instance, a separation agreement needs no particular set of words to be effective, although it generally follows the pattern of any formal legal contract. It is a document which 'belongs' to your client and her spouse in the sense that it can say anything they want it to say. The same is true of a cohabitation agreement. Try to write documents like this in straightforward phrases your client understands and will continue to understand when you are no longer there to explain. You may have to argue with the other lawyer if he feels safer sticking to time-worn phrases, but there is no restriction in law. Be careful not to create ambiguities; some archaic phrases are the way they are because they work, but do try to look at things with a fresh eye.

COUNSEL'S LANGUAGE

Barristers are often worse communicators than solicitors. If you accept the need to use simple language, you will be unlikely to continue to use counsel of the sort who retreats behind a barrage of technical, pompous language – which clients generally find very off-putting. Do not be afraid when you get a document settled by counsel to change the wording if you think it is obscure. This is often necessary where counsel has settled an affidavit for the client in tones of a Regius Professor. You may need to discuss some points with counsel and you must make sure that your rewrite gets the same point across. Make your view of the way things should be written clear to counsel so that you can work together in a co-operative effort.

STYLE

For most of us, good style does not come overnight; it needs working at. The pleasure of it is that it is always developing. You should aim for simplicity and clarity. If it looks effortless, so much the better.

PRESENTATION

The presentation of all your paperwork is one of the factors by which you will be judged, particularly by others in the profession and by the court. You therefore need to take the greatest possible care over both its content and the way that it looks.

To some extent, presentation is outside your control. Many firms have a house style which they impose on documents but, of course, whatever the style, the documents should look tidy and professional.

You may be at the other end of the spectrum, where the equipment and stationery you have to work with are so poor that it is difficult to make any document look good. There is scarcely any excuse for this with modern information technology, but you may have to lobby to improve standards.

However, even with limited technical resources it is possible to make any document leaving your office look clean and tidy.

The following procedures are small in themselves but speak volumes about the care you have given to the matter in hand.

- When a document is sewn up (which is now a dying art) make sure that the silk is kept flat and does not twist around.
- When you have large bundles of documents to send to counsel, they look better in a ring binder, and it makes it easier for counsel to read them. Some firms have binders ready printed in 'corporate' colours, but, if you do not have these resources, printed stick-on labels can produce a good effect and are much cheaper.
- Take trouble over layout and spacing, and emphasise to your secretary that this is something which you believe matters.
- Choose envelopes which are large enough for the documents they contain so that the documents do not have to be folded too much.
- Send reply paid envelopes of suitable size to your client when you want to be sure of getting a document back promptly.
- When you fill in a form, whether by hand or computer, try to keep it as tidy as possible, and fill it in by hand only if you have legible writing.
- Use cardboard corners to hold drafts together; they are much smarter and stronger than staples alone.

PETITIONS

There is nothing wrong with using a printed petition form, although it does look more professional if you have the whole thing typed out. You need to make sure that, if you use a form, it can be filled in neatly; some are better than others. Alternatively, you can produce a standard form to complete on the computer.

Where there are children, list them in order of age. (I once received a petition which named seven children in random age order, as though the petitioner had completely lost track of who they were.)

If behaviour is being cited, do not write a three-volume novel, or allow counsel to do so. Five or six paragraphs should be sufficient in all but the most extreme cases, and two or three sentences is usually enough in each paragraph. You may be sending a draft to the respondent's legal adviser for approval and so want to have enough material to shed some of it if there are objections. However, I would suggest that if you have drafted it carefully in the first place and have not been unduly provocative, it is unlikely to be reduced significantly. After all, if there is sufficient co-operation to look at the draft, the implication is that the divorce will not be contested, in principle. The more lengthy the allegations, the more the respondent may object to, and you could end up provoking the situation rather than assisting your client.

It is quite useful, when you start out, to collect some standard paragraphs which describe unreasonable behaviour. When you read a petition someone else has drafted and come across a particularly felicitous phrase, add a copy of it to your collection. This saves time groping for a suitable form of words. However, do not reuse these gems without making sure that they apply to your client and, where appropriate, introduce your own variations.

Be careful that the allegations of behaviour are 'pleaded' and not set out in narrative or anecdotal form. Make it clear that the behaviour complained of did distress your client; do not assume it is self-evident.

AFFIDAVIT IN SUPPORT OF THE PETITION

If you have time at the first interview, you may be able to run through the questions for the affidavit with your client, assuming that, at that stage, you know the basis on which you will be filing the petition. There are questions on the form which you will not automatically deal with at the first interview – especially when your client has been apart from her husband for some years – for example, what led up to the parting. Therefore, dealing with this at the first interview can save time later.

Do prepare a front sheet for the exhibited acknowledgement of service rather than typing or writing the words exhibiting the document at the top of the form. After all, with a computer, it can be set up in advance and there is only the cost of an extra piece of paper. There are two advantages – the exhibit is less likely to get lost and it looks more professional.

When you send your client the affidavit to swear, remember that if your client is in receipt of Legal Help you can be reimbursed for the oath fee and you should therefore send the fee to your client in advance. Some clients may otherwise find it hard to get the fee together and may thus delay swearing the oath. If your client does not have a bank account, it is probably better to send a postal order rather than a cheque.

FINANCIAL STATEMENTS

The following are obvious points, but are often overlooked.

- List outgoings by reference to the same period, ie per month, week or year, in one column on the right-hand side of the page so that anyone reading it gets a clear picture of your client's needs. Do not express some figures as weekly amounts and others as monthly, so that the reader has to calculate the totals for himself. Add the columns up, check the sums, and insert the total at the bottom of the column.

- Remember that one month is 4⅓ weeks, not 4; when your client gives you figures, check that she has not made this mistake. Figures for monthly expenditure which divide neatly by four should be queried by you in case they have been multiplied up from incorrect weekly figures.
- Where the figures are in a foreign currency, state the amount in that currency and what rate of exchange you are using, and use it to translate all the figures into pounds sterling so as to make it clear and unambiguous.

SWORN STATEMENTS SUPPORTING APPLICATIONS FOR DOMESTIC VIOLENCE INJUNCTIONS

The court needs to know why your client has made her application. Therefore, you need to deal with the incident which caused this specific application to be made as the first major part of the sworn statement, once you have established the basic facts.

After that it is probably best to give the history of the relationship from the beginning, listing previous occasions of violence, in chronological order. I have suggested that it is easier to get the client to recollect such incidents working backwards, but this makes for awkward reading; you should reverse the sequence of events when you write it out.

BRIEFS TO COUNSEL

It is important to make briefs to counsel look as good as possible. You are judged by these, and your reputation goes round the profession.

- Make sure that counsel has clear legible copies of all the documents.
- Make sure that they are in chronological order.
- Label enclosures clearly.
- Use dividers if you are sending the papers in a ring binder.
- Make sure that every page is copied on one side only and faces the front of the bundle.
- Correspondence should be in chronological order, with the earliest at the front, which generally means the other way round to your file.
- If you are using more than one ring binder, label each binder clearly and either use all the same colour (some firms have a house colour) or use different colours to distinguish the different parts of the paperwork, and make the distinction clear in your instructions.

- Always state on the front sheet the time and date of the hearing or conference so that it is clearly visible. Some people write it in red on the top left-hand corner of the front sheet.

Above all, take pride in the way your work looks. It can be an enormous source of satisfaction in itself if it is done properly and can earn you the praise and respect of counsel and judges.

SUMMARY

- Think carefully about the way in which you communicate.
- Keep your language simple.
- Be brief.
- Aim for clarity.
- Use standard English, not 'Lawyerspeak'.
- Good presentation is vital. Take trouble over it.
- Aim for tidy, well-presented documents.

Chapter 6

CHILDREN

You owe an obvious duty of care to a parent: the client sitting before you. But you also owe a duty to the children. Children are your invisible clients. You need to give thought to their situation in the family break-up and remember the impact your actions and advice will have on their young lives.

Your task is made more difficult because you cannot assume, as you might have done in other circumstances, that your client will necessarily have the children's needs as her first priority. The stress and unhappiness of divorce and family breakdown often cause diminished ability to act as a good parent. Every matrimonial solicitor will tell you of clients who say that the children have not noticed anything wrong, or that they have not really been affected by the break-up. But this is hardly ever the case. If your client says something like this you can be privately sceptical about her assessment of the children's reaction. It may be that the break-up is making your client intensely introspective, to the point where she has not observed her children closely, or is refusing to admit to herself what she has observed because it would only add to the pain she is experiencing.

There are so many things to discuss with your client at the first interview that it is easy to forget about the children, especially if your client's most immediate worry is the division of property. A good way of ensuring that you spend adequate time discussing the children, if your client has not raised the issue already, is to pause when you get to the point of asking routine questions about the children and discuss them in more detail. If your client says that the children are not affected, you need to explain that in all probability they are, or soon will be, but that children are often careful to disguise their feelings in front of their parents.

There are several suggestions you can make to clients as ways of dealing with, or pre-empting, the problems that may arise. I have found that the following are helpful.

- Parents should tell their children's schools what is happening at home. A lot of clients do not think to do this, or are put off by the idea of letting the schools know about their private lives, but it does help the school to be understanding if a child's behaviour or standard of work changes.

- Warn your client that children's school work often does suffer, but, with encouragement and understanding displayed by both parents, most children can and will pick up again.

- Children, particularly younger ones, often think of human relationships in terms of rules rather than choices; they think that parents *have* to love each other and their children because that is part of the order of things. When they realise that Daddy does not love Mummy any more, they begin to wonder whether other rules are broken too, and they may worry that their parents will not love them any more. They will need constant reassurance from both parents that this love is still there.

- Children start to try out things to see what other rules have been wiped out, eg bed-times and table manners. Parents who feel guilty for what they have done to their children may start to relax these rules because they feel sorry and because they do not want to seem too strict. This can lead to spoiling the children, bad behaviour and loss of temper all round. If you alert your client to this danger, it can help her to spot the signs and act sensibly.

CONTACT VISITS

Clients need to be sensible and sensitive over visiting arrangements. By the time you see your client, arrangements may already have been made, and may be working well. Nevertheless, find out what the present arrangements are and if there are any aspects you know that may lead to problems. Warn your client gently about these but do not panic her into making dramatic changes which may upset everyone. For instance, where a parent who has recently left the house is seeing the children several times a week, after a while this may become difficult, for both parents as well as for the children. You do not want to discourage a good relationship, but you may need to point out that sometimes such arrangements need to tail off after a while and be replaced by a regular pattern of less frequent visits.

In these cases, you cannot lay down rules. No one knows what the ideal pattern of visiting is for children; every family needs to work it out for itself. This is not an easy task. Many clients give the impression that they would like you, as the expert, to lay down the rules for them. This is not something that you can do, and you have to be wary of appearing so knowledgeable that you sap your client's confidence in her own ability to make decisions. Some of the following however may be helpful suggestions.

- Children need their own time. As they grow older their lives are filled with activities – swimming, dancing, riding, Cubs, Brownies, and socialising with their friends. Parents need to respect this and allow for it in their visiting arrangements. The converse of this is that the parent with whom the child lives should make sure that the child's life is not cluttered up with so many activities that there is no time left for visits to the other parent.

- Timekeeping seems to be the single most annoying thing about visiting arrangements. If times are agreed they must be kept. If they turn out to be impractical, they ought to be changed, otherwise they can become the focus for all the bitterness in the relationship between the parents. Try to make your client appreciate this. If your client is the parent with visiting rights, you may need to explain to him how difficult children find unpunctuality. Fifteen or even five minutes may seem like an eternity to a child who is waiting to be picked up for an outing. If a parent is late bringing the child back, this too may be very upsetting for the child, who is aware that it will annoy and worry his mother. Now that nearly everyone seems to carry a mobile phone, there should be less excuse for the unexplained late arrival.
- 'Contact is the child's right to see the parent, not the other way round.' Using this phrase may make it easier to explain the position to parents. It is a useful way of expressing the law because it enables you to change the way in which your client may perceive the situation. Sometimes you will need to use it to redress the balance of power in favour of a child whose feelings and needs are being totally disregarded by his parents.
- A year planner with coloured stickers such as spots or stars can be useful for the whole family. The child can keep it at his home and mark up the visits that have been arranged. This helps everyone to plan ahead and the child can take an active part. It should also help to stop arguments about ambiguous arrangements.
- Children's needs for visits will change as they grow up. It is important that arrangements made now do not become so rigid that they cause difficulties in later years. Visiting times may need to expand or become less frequent to suit the children.

If your client is reluctant to agree to visits at an early stage and you consider that her reasons are not ones which a court would support so that she is likely to have a solution imposed on her, it is not very productive to say 'Well, you'll have to let your husband have visiting arrangements or the court will make you'. This encourages your client to adopt a Joan of Arc-like stance and she may use that ominous phrase 'You're obviously on his side ...'. You need a strategy which gets her used to the idea of visits gradually. There are lots of ways of doing this, starting with things like supervised visits or short visits on familiar territory, which gradually build up to longer ones. Try to work out a timetable with a progression of visits, so that, on the assumption that the child reacts favourably, visiting time will gradually increase. This helps your client and the child avoid the conflict which is otherwise bound to arise. It may help you to note the agreed timetable at the front of your file so that you can check how things are going from time to time.

It is worth warning clients that children tend to get overwrought after visits, even in the best-regulated families, but this does not mean the visits are doing them any harm. You can point out that even the most cheerful of children at the end of a day visiting friends or relatives can become fractious when they get home. Excitement and tiredness cause this as much as anything else. In the normal course of events you would just jolly them along and try to calm them down for bed. The emotions divorce arouses can make all this seem a lot worse; your client will need to try to stay as calm as possible so that the children do not pick up her emotions and react to them in their tiredness.

'Visiting' parents often worry about the amount of contact they are having with their children, and some are quite insistent that the children should be shared out equally. This is not a principle which the court will support in any event but it may be hard for you to make the point that it is the *quality* of the time and the relationship that matter to the child, rather than the amount of time he spends with your client. It may help your client if you ask him to recollect the relationships he had with adults when he was a child. Most of us can recall feeling very close to some adults whom we did not see very often, such as grandparents or godparents, precisely because of the interest they took in us and our absolute faith in their love for us.

MEDIATION

In some cases you may feel that your client would be best helped by another agency such as a mediation service. (I have dealt with using other agencies in Chapter 4, and you will need to consider the things I said there.) In particular, cases involving children seem to benefit from such services. But in some cases a meeting at your office may help to resolve matters, as suggested in Chapter 9.

HEARINGS

If it looks as though you will end up in court for a full hearing on matters relating to the children, it is worth stressing to your client that in such situations it is rare for either party to end up with exactly what he or she wants. The court (except in extreme circumstances) always looks to find a middle way. Your client should also be aware that an imposed solution is generally harder to live with than one which she and her husband have worked out for themselves. For some clients, however, an arrangement imposed on them by the court is the only answer, and there comes a point where it is useless for you to try to find another solution.

If you are going to proceed to a hearing, do resist the temptation to cram your client's statements full of minor incidents of aggravation, much as your client may want you to. They can often result in making your client look like the really difficult party. Point out to a client who is spoiling for a fight that there is life after litigation, and that she and the father have to continue being parents for the rest of their lives, until they are grandparents and even great-grandparents. (Some of them will not have thought of this until you mention it.)

BRINGING THE CHILDREN TO COURT

Occasionally, the court may require the children to come to a hearing. This may be laid down as part of the standard procedural directions, as it is at the Divorce Registry for the initial directions appointment. The children may be sent for on the day of a hearing; I have even known a judge do this in the middle of an application for an injunction.

Whenever possible warn your client so that she can prepare the children. It can be strange and frightening for children, especially as few courts have adequate facilities for them, or even suitable places for them to sit. Make sure that your client brings something to keep them quietly amused, eg books, comics or games which do not have little pieces that go all over the floor, or a comforting teddy. They may have to hang around, so drinks and refreshments are also a good idea. It does no harm for you to have armed yourself with useful things too. Sweets may help if the parents have no objection. How good are you at paper folding . . .?

If you have to bring the children to court unexpectedly you may have to take them out of school and send somebody to collect them. If your client is going to do this, make sure that she does not panic the children on the way back, or indeed try to coach them in what they should say. If in doubt, go with her, or send a reliable colleague.

Many lawyers feel uneasy about having any contact with the children. This stems partly from a feeling that the children should be involved in the proceedings as little as possible, and partly from embarrassment. You need to overcome this if you are placed in a situation where you have to meet the children. It is much worse for them if you try to pretend that they are not there. Be polite to them, formal but friendly. Children appreciate being treated in a 'grown-up' manner. Be kind and speak to them gently. Try to anticipate what their fears may be and allay them. Give them a chance to ask you questions. Remember that for most children the idea of court means police and prison and they need to be told that no one is going to be locked away. If they are small, bob down to their level, or sit them up on chairs so that you can talk face to face. Avoid being an alarming black and white pillar.

CHILDREN IN DANGER

What should you do if your client tells you that he intends to commit an offence in connection with a child, such as kidnapping or sexual abuse? You owe your client a duty of confidentiality and his communications to you are privileged. On the other hand the child is vulnerable and you may be the only adult in a position to protect the child.

The Law Society's Family Law Committee used to publish some guidelines on the topic, although these no longer appear as a separate annex in the *Guide to the Professional Conduct of Solicitors*. In summary, it stated that your immediate duty is to your client, and part of that duty is to make sure that your client knows the legal position, so if he intimates to you that he intends to commit a criminal offence you should tell him about this and warn him of the possible consequences. As a lawyer you cannot connive at the committing of a crime and, if a client tries to enlist your help in doing so, these communications take him outside the bounds of the normal solicitor/client relationship and are no longer privileged. This means that you can pass them on to a third party, such as the police.

In exceptional cases, the *Guide* (at Chapter 16.02, Note 4) states that confidentiality can be breached, but it is left to your judgment as a solicitor in any particular case as to whether you think the public interest in preventing an offence outweighs your duty to your client. This is not something to decide on your own; you will need to discuss it with other people in the office who have wider experience than you. If there is no one to whom you can turn, consider discussing it with a practitioner you know and trust (and is not involved in the case), or contact the Ethics and Guidance department of The Law Society, which has always, in my experience, proved to be most sensitive and thoughtful in its advice.

In practice, when your client tells you something which sets your mental alarm bells ringing what should you do? First of all, try to relax and talk to your client sensibly. When a client walked into my office with his small daughter in tow, whom he had taken from her mother, I was aghast. 'You can't do that!' I said; he immediately decided that I was not 'on his side' and I had to spend a long time convincing him that I would act to the best of my ability for him.

Without saying anything to give the impression that you think that your client is acting laudably, you can still get your client to tell his side of the story and find out what is motivating him. This is important because your immediate impression that your client is about to do, or has done, something illegal, may also be wrong. Parents sometimes 'kidnap' their children for the best of motives – if, for instance, they believe the child to be in danger and have not been able to think of any other way to provide immediate protection. All your instincts, as a lawyer, will be to condemn the idea of people taking the law into their own hands, but it is possible that your client has acted with the best of motives. Make sure first that you have fully understood the story and taken a full note.

Many situations which at first present themselves as though a crime of abduction is about to be, or has been, committed, arise because the tensions in the family have reached such a crisis that dramatic action seems to your client to be the only solution. You can often act to defuse these tensions and establish lines of communication and conciliation.

In circumstances where your client has taken children from his spouse and you feel that he will have to restore them to her because any application on his part is going to be hopeless, you can help to get the children back if your client has the legal position explained to him and realises that your suggestion is the best way to proceed. You can telephone the mother, or her solicitor if you are already in communication, and make suitable arrangements. You may also be able to negotiate visits to the child or a meeting with the other parent to sort out your client's concerns.

If you feel that you have to breach the confidence of your client you should explain this to him, unless this will mean that the risk to the child is increased.

KEEPING IN TOUCH

Even where there is no dispute over the children it is essential not to overlook their existence as the case progresses. Always consider their position in the proceedings. Ask about them and how they are. This is more than just a courtesy between you and your client; it can also help you to nip problems in the bud.

SUMMARY

- Children should come first, as legal and moral considerations.
- Discuss difficulties with clients in detail.
- Give your client helpful pointers for coping with visits and other difficulties.
- Be alive to the possibilities of mediation.
- Avoid making allegations about behaviour which only make things worse between the clients; they have to go on being parents.
- If children have to come to court, make special arrangements for them.
- Never forget that the children are part of the case.

Chapter 7

FINANCIAL APPLICATIONS

It is not the purpose of this chapter to discuss the issue of quantum, or even to rehearse the procedural rules which you have to follow. There are plenty of good books to which you can refer for that. Instead, I suggest ways of approaching financial negotiations and applications which are of practical help.

START EARLY

As financial matters are ancillary to the main suit it is tempting to put off the consideration of these issues until the divorce proceedings (or separation negotiations) are well under way. If you have to apply for public funding to cover these matters for your client, this adds to the temptation to delay and, indeed, in these circumstances you have little choice. Any time-consuming matters may have to wait until the grant of public funding if you are to be paid. Unfortunately, this can mean that you do not really think about the issues involved until a late stage, and this can cause problems because it may restrict the available options.

From the first appointment with your client you should begin to consider what the financial outcome is likely to be, what permutations are possible and what your client wants to achieve. You have to do this before you can consider how to run the case in order to achieve your objectives.

INFORMATION GATHERING

You are in no position to make a proper judgment about the likely outcome of the case without detailed financial information. You can often sketch an answer for your client at a first meeting, but you will have to make it clear that this can only be a provisional judgment and may well change in the light of information received later in the case. The sooner you can gather this information, the sooner you can feel more confident about your judgment and give your client a better estimate of what is likely to happen.

To a large extent you are in your client's hands. You cannot force him to tell you everything or produce all the documents you need as quickly as you would like them. Some clients are models of dispatch. Others take longer; some perhaps because they are inefficient, but more, I suspect, because they find the divorce distressing to the point where they would rather do anything than read one of your letters and act on its contents.

FULL AND FRANK DISCLOSURE

Full and frank disclosure is a very useful phrase for explaining to your client what is expected of him. It is important to stress that it is mutual; your client's spouse will have to do the same. Many clients are very reluctant to produce the necessary information and you may have to stress that it is not your personal crusade but a principle which is upheld by the court.

How do you get this information? Your technique will depend on your client. Some know all about their finances; they keep tidy files which put yours to shame, full of bills and bank statements. Others have little or no idea; they have never calculated a budget, and if they keep any papers they are in a terrible mess. I once asked a client to bring me in all the papers that he could find so that I could sort them out for him. He brought in three black plastic dustbin bags, full of all sorts of things, some in an advanced state of decay. I have worded such requests very carefully ever since.

It is best to get the client to do most of the initial work. You do not have the time, and your client would have difficulty in affording the costs if you did. Further, your client is very often in a better position than you to gather the information. For instance, he can write direct to his bank or credit card agency; you will have to get him to sign letters of authority if you approach them yourself. This puts the onus of timing on your client, and this is no bad thing. Sometimes solicitors can proceed too quickly for their clients, who need time to adjust to their new status. If your client wants matters to progress quickly he will get the information quickly; if he takes a long time you can make it clear to him that it is his responsibility. You have to keep a weather eye out to make sure that things are not dragging so slowly that your client is actually harming his case, but there is a limit to the amount of pressure you can apply. There are clients, however, who are not capable of doing the information-gathering exercise themselves. If, for example, your client is not literate or articulate enough, you will have to help him.

It is not enough just to tell your client that you need to know everything about his financial position and expect him to let you have that information in an acceptable form. He may not know what you want; he may leave out things which you regard as crucial, but which he thinks are immaterial, perhaps because he and his wife have always had an understanding that a particular piece of property belongs to him. The wife's solicitors are not likely to be convinced by this kind of explanation.

Form E has made the task of gathering and collating the information easier. Some clients can simply be given a blank form and encouraged to get on with it. The disadvantage is that some clients find forms very difficult to fill in and you may store up more work for yourself in the long run. If you do use Form E, you need to make sure that you mark it up so that it fits your client's lifestyle. Go through it in advance, deleting those sections that do not apply, so that it is less daunting. For some clients it is best to send a list of the documents that you want them to obtain so that you can use them to compile a Form E (see Appendix 7A).

It is useful to ask your client to complete a separate list of outgoings (see Appendix 7B). This will prompt him to remember all the things he has to afford since Form E does not list possible items of expenditure. In many cases you can hand this to your client at your first meeting and ask him to let you have it back as soon as possible. Again, you may need to edit it to tailor it to your client's lifestyle; the easiest way of doing this is to cross out the things you know will not apply.

DISCLOSING THE INFORMATION

The pre-application protocol sets out in formal fashion the suggestions that I made for early disclosure in the first edition of this book, so there is little more to say, apart from a word of warning. Do not swallow your client's answers to the questions on the form wholesale without checking them and doing the sums yourself.

I once read an affidavit in which solicitors had simply written down what their client told them about his income and outgoings and had not checked them against the bank and credit card statements that were exhibited. These showed that his outgoings on such inessentials as hobbies and drink far exceeded the amount he was being asked to pay to his son, which he claimed he could not afford. The moral is to make sure that the information you send out will stand up to close examination. It is very embarrassing when your client's confident assertion, relayed by you, turns out to have been, at best, wishful thinking on his part.

If you find an inconsistency in the information your client has supplied to you, you must raise it with your client, but do so tactfully. Do not suggest that your client has been 'economical with the truth', but tell him that this is the sort of thing his wife's advisers will pick up and that it is prudent to explain it in advance.

FORM WHICH DISCLOSURE SHOULD TAKE

In cases where my client's affairs are complicated, I have found that it is quite effective to make disclosure of documents in a separate document with a summary at the front, dealing first with income, and then with capital. In this document, I refer to the numerous enclosures which support the statement by number. The enclosures can be bound behind the statement in a binder with coloured dividers so that they are easily identified. This helps me as well as the other solicitors because the copy I keep is then an organised way of retaining all the pieces of paper the client has given me.

If the bundle is thick I generally keep it in a ring binder, which makes it easier for copying later. It looks very smart if the copies you send out are bound with commercial binding equipment. Information which is presented clearly is less likely to provoke a barrage of enquiries than information which is parcelled out and given in a scrappy fashion. Inefficiency can be construed as deception.

It is a golden rule that you do not send out information about your client without thoroughly understanding it first. If your client's affairs are complicated, it is tempting to write down what is told to you and let the other side work it out for themselves. But if you do not understand your client's position, you cannot advise him properly. At the risk of appearing an idiot to your client, who may be a whizz with figures, go over the information with him until you are sure that you have grasped it thoroughly and can set it out in a straightforward statement or affidavit. Do not assume that counsel or an accountant will work it out for you. Remember that most matrimonial lawyers are not experts with figures, neither are judges; if you do not explain things properly there is a risk of misunderstandings and ambiguities which may damage your client. But do not underestimate your own ability to grasp complex facts. The information and experience you get from one difficult case will inform your handling of the next case and broaden your professional development and experience.

The obvious advantage of organising your client's disclosure is that it clarifies matters for everyone and provides you with an excellent basis for a court bundle if you need one later.

TIMING THE APPLICATION

It is up to you to decide on the most opportune time to lodge your application for ancillary relief. Some factors which are beyond your control, such as the granting of public funding, will inevitably influence this, but, if there are no such constraints, when should you do it?

In order to decide this you have to do a balancing exercise, weighing up the costs you will incur in preparing the application and Form E against the possibility that there may be a settlement and your effort may have been wasted.

In nearly every case you will want some degree of financial disclosure before you can settle. Clearly, if this is forthcoming promptly and appears to be a model of candour, the need to file ancillary proceedings recedes. However, if disclosure is slow and piecemeal, it may be better to impose the court's framework on the discussions sooner rather than later. You can hesitate to do this, particularly when the parties are friendly, because you do not want it to be interpreted as a hostile act, but I have seen too many cases where the hope of settlement and inertia on the part of the potential applicant's lawyers have combined to allow the matter to run for months or even years before it eventually reaches court. The 'new' ancillary relief procedures are deliberately designed to deal with this issue and encourage people to achieve a settlement by one route or another.

It is much more difficult to get full and frank disclosure if you leave your application too long; dishonest parties may take advantage of the time-lag to conceal assets, and events may intervene which change the parties' circumstances so that you have to change your initial advice radically. This may annoy your clients and can make them lose all faith in you. If you let the momentum lapse it will increase the costs. Therefore, if there is likely to be an application for ancilliary relief, start working on the Form E as soon as possible unless the case is obviously going to settle. Hope may spring eternal in the human breast, but solicitors had better temper that hope with a good dose of healthy realism. If your client is waiting for public funding, encourage her to do as much as she can to get the necessary information together in the ways I have suggested above. You will then be ready to proceed as soon as the funding certificate is issued.

TAKING THE CASE FURTHER

Once you have filed your client's application – or the other party has done so – you are locked into the court's timetable. Make sure that your client understands this, and how vital it is to keep to the dates set. It can be helpful to issue each client with a diary sheet for the next few months showing the deadlines and when appointments are likely to happen. You don't want them booking their holidays in the middle of it all.

One of the keys to successful litigation is to keep the momentum going. Do not let the file languish in the drawer. Always be mindful of what is to be done next. Have a clear timetable for what needs to be done and when it is likely to happen and mark your diary up so that time limits are not exceeded. One of my wise colleagues used to say that files do not make any money for you while they are in the cabinet, and this is solid advice. The policy should be to keep the files moving. If you are dealing with publicly funded cases, a high turnover of work is essential in order to make a profit. However, more importantly, it has the added benefit of serving the best interests of your client.

DISCOVERY

When you succeed in getting the documents you have requested, examine them closely. Check bank statements and credit card statements in detail; they can often be very revealing. In some cases you may want to leave this to counsel to avoid duplicating effort; if you do so, make it clear in your instructions that you have not analysed the findings and you want counsel to do it. You should do this at an early stage so that you can ask further questions if necessary. Do not leave it until the run-up to trial only to find that counsel wants you to obtain items which were readily available some time ago.

USING EXPERTS

In some cases you may need expert witnesses, such as property valuers or medical experts, but their involvement is limited. The experts who become most commonly involved are accountants, who are brought in to carry out a forensic analysis of your client's or her spouse's financial affairs.

It is usually counsel who suggests the use of such a person. If you have a barrister in the case I would not normally instruct an expert without a prior discussion with counsel, and, of course, liaison with the other party's lawyers. Counsel may also know more about who the most useful experts are, having seen them in previous cases.

Forensic accountants are not cheap. Their hourly rate will often be more than yours. You should, of course, find out what they charge at the outset, just as you should, as a matter of good practice, tell your client what your own charges will be. The cost of instructing expert witnesses must be carefully analysed by the solicitors for both spouses and counsel. Is it worth it? Do not rush into instructing an expert, but consider whether it is necessary at an early stage of the case, bearing in mind the costs compared with the possible advantages for your client.

If you do instruct an expert he will need a full set of instructions, much as you would for a brief to counsel. Clearly, where an expert is instructed jointly, you must agree these instructions with the other party's lawyers. If you are instructing an accountant let him have a full set of the documents available, including any correspondence which has financial relevance. State clearly what you are looking for, but also ask the expert to see whether he feels that there are any other angles which should be explored and which you have missed.

Keep your client fully involved because there may be some information she has not given you which suddenly illuminates something that has puzzled your expert.

CALDERBANK LETTERS

At some point you may have to consider whether you should make a *Calderbank* offer. *Calderbank* offers have taken on a rather talismanic sheen. 'We'll send them a *Calderbank* letter' is said in a manner which suggests that all will be well after that, and the other side will come to heel quickly. They are undoubtedly useful and can help to resolve cases, but I believe that they are too often credited with more power than they actually have, and sometimes clients can be deeply disappointed at the results.

When and how to make a *Calderbank* offer

It is not advisable to make a *Calderbank* offer until there has been full disclosure from both sides. You should wait at least until you have had full disclosure from the other side. If you make a *Calderbank* offer before you have reciprocated with full information, you lay yourself open to the argument that the other side could not possibly consider it without essential information from you. You have thus negated any advantage the letter might have given you. For much the same reasons, it is considered prudent to include an offer to pay some or all of the other side's costs, otherwise they could argue that the absence of such an offer means that they are compelled to continue with the litigation.

The letter should be clear and detailed and should deal with all the matters at issue between the parties. If some matters are already agreed they should be included in the letter. This ensures that if you have to produce it to the court, the judge can see clearly that all the matters which would have been in a final order are covered; otherwise you will have to produce a bundle of correspondence which is messy and has much less impact.

The letter should state clearly that it is a *Calderbank* letter. There are several standard ways of wording this. In addition, it should state at the top: 'Without prejudice, save as to costs'.

Problems

Beware of misleading your client into thinking that the *Calderbank* letter will give total protection against costs, since this is not the case in the majority of matrimonial proceedings. This is because, generally, there is not enough money to go round and, if the effect of the *Calderbank* letter is to make the wife pay costs out of the money she needs for rehousing herself and the children, the court may be reluctant to allow the letter to have such an effect and, in order to avoid this, judges will often try to find reasons for restricting the protective effect of the letter. I have known awards which have differed so slightly from the *Calderbank* offer that in practical terms little difference has been made, but the judge has seized on these slight differences and disregarded the offer.

You must also consider the application of Family Proceedings Rules 1991, r 2.69C and the risk of your client, if she is the applicant, doing worse than the original offer and her counter-proposal. You clearly need to explain to your client the risk she runs in costs, but at the same time not frighten her so much that she will hesitate to make any sensible claim.

It is arguable that in cases where both sides are publicly funded *Calderbank* letters have no place because an order for costs from one party to the other is unlikely.

Good points

There is undoubtedly a need to consider whether a case is able to be settled and, if so, on what terms. If an offer is made which is the product of considerable thought and reasoned argument and which has taken the best points of both parties' cases into account, it can be the breakthrough which everyone desires.

Clearly, in some cases the *Calderbank* offer has the beneficial effect of protecting the party who has made it as far as the subsequent costs are concerned. Even in publicly funded cases, where the benefits are not guaranteed, there is a useful place for such offers because of their status. If a *Calderbank* offer is made it is the solicitor's duty to consider it carefully and explore the ramifications of it in detail with his client.

SETTLEMENT

If you do settle a case you will need to agree a draft consent order, or minutes of order, to be submitted to the court. The convention seems to be that the applicant's solicitor writes the first draft, but this is not always the case. It may be that you have more time than the other legal adviser, and so it is agreed that you will do it. In some cases, experience will have taught you that the other legal adviser cannot be relied upon to produce anything suitable, and you might as well do it yourself rather than wait for his attempt and then have to rewrite it.

In any event, there is no excuse for poorly written draft orders. There are good precedents available, notably the one produced by the Solicitors Family Law Association. Courts seem to have given general approval to the clauses set out in that precedent, so you have the reassurance of knowing that the judge is not likely to take exception to your grammar and send the whole thing back.

It is worth taking time and trouble over draft orders, making sure that they are not ambiguous and that they cover future eventualities. There are some golden rules, like expressing the shares in the house as percentages in case a change in the property market renders the original calculations unworkable. Remember that the powers of the court are limited. Matters which the court cannot order the parties to do, such as payment of maintenance by standing order, have to go in the preamble to the undertakings.

When you submit the draft order to the court both parties should have completed Form M1. You should have a copy of the other party's details before the order goes to the court and they should have yours. This is because the basic purpose of such statements is a last-minute check that there has been proper disclosure on both sides, following the case of *Jenkins v Livesey (formerly Jenkins)* [1985] FLR 813. There is no point in either side filling in the statement if they are not exchanged.

Make sure that your client sees a draft of the order at an early stage, and take the trouble to send her a detailed explanatory letter with it so that she can understand it. Explain why it falls into two parts. If you have drafted anything based on assumptions rather than actual instructions, check this aspect with her specifically. Never overlook the possibility that your client may find the length of the document and the legal language so impenetrable that she may not bother to check it. If you have doubts about whether your client is able to understand the document, make an appointment with her so that you can go through it together carefully.

When the order is returned from the court, check it carefully against the draft. Mistakes occur quite often. If you spot them soon enough they can be put right under the 'slip rule', but if they go undetected for years it can be difficult to correct them.

Make sure that your client has a copy of the order, and impress on her that it is an important document which should be kept. If other people need copies of the order, such as conveyancing solicitors, send them out yourself, rather than relying on your client to make and distribute the copies.

SUMMARY

- Start action early and plan your strategy.
- Gather information thoroughly.
- Disclose information systematically.
- Issue proceedings early rather than later.
- Consider *Calderbank* letters carefully.
- Take trouble over draft orders.

APPENDIX 7A

CHECKLIST OF DOCUMENTS

When you come to your next appointment with me please bring with you the following documents if they apply to your financial situation.

- Electricity bills for the last 12 months
- Gas bills for the last 12 months
- Telephone bills for the last 12 months
- Water rate demand for the last 12 months
- Council tax demand for the last 12 months

If you don't have these you can ring up the authority concerned and they will generally give you the figures over the phone.

- Rent book
- Mortgage account showing amounts outstanding
- Insurance policies
- HP agreements
- Loan agreements
- Bank statements for the last 12 months (your bank will keep copies if you have lost the ones that were sent to you)
- Building Society passbooks
- Any other documents which are proof of amounts of money you have to pay regularly

APPENDIX 7B

PRESENT OUTGOINGS

Please fill this in as accurately as you possibly can to show your outgoings at present. If you know that some items are going to change shortly please give both the present figure and the projected figure.

The right-hand column should show monthly figures only.

There are spaces for working out the monthly figure by most items. A month is 4.33 weeks, not just 4.

Please find old bills where possible and put them with this questionnaire when you give it back.

Cross out the items which are not a part of your family budget.

If someone pays for any of these items for you, please fill in the figure and mark that item clearly showing who pays for it.

ACCOMMODATION COSTS	£ per month
Mortgage/Rent	....
Endowment policy linked to mortgage	....
Council Tax	....
Water rates: £........ per ½ yr. ÷ 6 =	....
Electricity	
add last 4 ¼s and ÷ 12 =	....
Gas	
add last 4 ¼s and ÷ 12 =	....
Telephone: £........ per ¼ ÷ 3 =	....
Service Charge	....
Ground Rent	....
Oil/Solid fuel	....

HOUSEHOLD EXPENSES	
Food/housekeeping	
£........ per week × 4·33 =	....
House insurance: £........ per yr. ÷ 12 =	....
Contents insurance	
£........ per yr. ÷ 12 =	....

	£ per month
Repairs/service contracts £........ per yr. ÷ 12 =	....
Cleaner £........ per week × 4·33 =	....
TV licence £........ per yr. ÷ 12 =	....
TV/video hire	....
Gardener £........ per week × no wks. worked per yr. ÷ 12 =	
	....
Other items (please list)	....

CAR

Insurance £........ per yr. ÷ 12 =	....
Road tax £........ per yr. ÷ 12 =	....
Car maintenance £........ per yr. ÷ 12 =	....
Petrol £........ per week × 4·33 =	....
Loan for car purchase (state when it will end ....)	....

CHILDREN

School expenses

I have assumed a total of 30 weeks of school a year. If the terms are longer or shorter please adjust the calculations accordingly.

Travel to school

£........ per wk. × 30 = ... ÷ 12 = ...

School dinners

£........ per wk. × 30 = ... ÷ 12 = ...

Uniforms £........ per yr. ÷ 12 = ...

Outings and trips

£........ per yr. ÷ 12 = ...

School fees

£........ per term × 3 ÷ 12 = ...

Other school expenses (please list)   ....

....

....

....

Private lessons
  please list, with costs ....
  ....
  ....
  ....

Out of school
Leisure activities (ballet, football, etc)
  please list, with costs ....
  ....
  ....
  ....

Clothes and shoes
  £........ per yr. ÷ 12 = ...
Nappies ....
Doctor ....
Dentist ....
Optician ....
Childminder/nanny
  £........ per wk. × 4·33 = ...
Hairdressing ....
Books ....
Toys ....
Christmas/birthdays ....
Other items (please list) ....

YOUR EXPENSES

Clothes and shoes

£........ per yr. ÷ 12 = ...

Hairdressing   ....

Doctor   ....

Dentist   ....

Optician   ....

Prescription charges   ....

Dry cleaning   ....

Entertainment   ....

Travel to work   ....

Lunches at work

£........ per wk. × 4·33 = ...

Holidays (including children if appropriate)

                                                       ....

Legal costs (if making a regular contribution to private
   costs or Legal Aid)

                                                       ....

Subscriptions (please list)   ....

OTHER ACCOMMODATION

(If, you are paying out for another property, please list
   what expenses you have for that property)

                                                       ....

                                                       ....

                                                       ....

                                                       ....

Other items (please list)   ....

                                                       ....

                                                       ....

                                                       ....

                                                       ....

CREDIT ARRANGEMENTS

Monthly
repayment
£

Please list in the appropriate columns:

HP AND OTHER LOANS

Creditor	*Item*	*Amount still outstanding*	
			....
			....
			....

CREDIT AND CHARGE CARDS

Card	*Total amount owing*	*What do you use it to buy generally?*	
			....
			....
			....

Chapter 8

INJUNCTIONS AND EMERGENCIES

When a client needs an emergency remedy, how do you react? Do you feel excited, enjoying the rush of adrenalin and the increased activity? Or do you get palpitations and feel ill, paralysed by the need to rush into action but terrified because you are not sure what to do?

To a large extent your reaction is going to depend on your temperament, and there is not much you can do to alter that. If you know you are the sort of person who is upset by such excitement, you can take a number of steps to help face the challenge without going into a flat spin. If you enjoy the urgency of such situations you also need to take care as well. It is easy to get carried away by the heightened atmosphere and rush off to court without having first considered whether your client's best interests are served by doing so.

The techniques I have suggested elsewhere in this book for dealing with your file and your client are of even greater importance when you are faced with the need to take emergency action on behalf of your client. Such action disrupts your whole pattern of working. Your carefully planned schedule for the day goes to pieces, your other clients have to take a back seat, you have to work for a long concentrated period on the same file, and you have to do everything as quickly as you can, without forgetting essential details.

INJUNCTION KIT

It helps to assemble what I call an injunction kit. Practitioners who frequently have to make applications for injunctions will clearly find this useful, but it is possibly more useful if this is not something that you have to do regularly because you will not be so familiar with what you ought to be doing. If you have been able to study the kit beforehand in a moment of comparative tranquillity, you will be better equipped to deal with an emergency.

STANDARD LETTERS

Standard letters and documents form a large part of this kit. They save valuable time which you would otherwise have to spend drafting and dictating. You can work out as many options as you think sensible, including the following:

- a letter to the process servers listing the documents you are enclosing and telling them how to serve the respondent and by what date;
- a form to give details describing the respondent, which can accompany the letter to the process servers;
- a letter to the local police station, telling them that you have obtained an injunction with a power of arrest and telling them what to do if the injunction is breached;
- a letter to your client's doctor asking him to do a report on the injuries sustained by your client;
- a letter from your client giving her authority to the doctor to reveal such matters to you.

USEFUL TELEPHONE NUMBERS

Bit by bit you will build up a list of useful telephone numbers, but some are worth looking up in advance so that you do not spend extra time searching for them. Numbers for local police stations, DSS offices, housing offices, social services offices, and women's refuges fall into this category. You may need to ring all or any of these on your client's behalf. There may also be other organisations in your area which may be able to help your client. As you start to contact these offices you will establish within them some very helpful personal contacts and can add their names to your dossier. This is often very useful because you are trying to galvanise large offices into emergency action, and sometimes the only way to do this is to beg for 'a favour', which is more likely to be forthcoming if you know the person at the other end of the telephone.

PRECEDENTS

The standard forms for a domestic violence injunction should be easily to hand, so that you have them all available. The client's supporting statement can also be prepared, to the extent of the heading and opening paragraph, and it is useful to have a checklist of the factors the court needs to take into account and which you therefore have to cover in that statement (see *Family Lawyer's Transaction Pack* (Family Law, 3rd edn, 2000).

Do not forget that there are other injunctions you may need to deal with, chief among these being s 37 applications to prevent disposal of assets. A pack of forms and precedents for this saves valuable time.

PRACTICE DIRECTIONS

It helps to avoid panic and wasted time if you already have copies of the relevant directions on such matters as preventing children leaving the jurisdiction. These things can be awkward to track down in the index of textbooks, particularly when you are in a rush.

TAKING YOUR CLIENT'S STATEMENT

If your injunction kit is assembled, it cuts down on the paperwork you will have to do and you can spend the time where it really counts, in taking down a detailed statement from your client. I have already suggested that the best way to proceed is to start with the most recent events and then work backwards, as clients seem to find it easier to recall things that way.

When you are dealing with allegations of violence, take your client through the story in considerable detail. If her partner opposes the application, she may be cross-examined thoroughly on what she says and so you need to test the story yourself. If your client has sustained an unprovoked attack, the court's approach will differ considerably from a case where she has received her injuries as the result of a violent quarrel where both parties have been hitting each other. If her description of what happened is not clear, get her to move about your room showing you what happened. This often helps her recollection anyway.

If offensive language accompanied the violence (and it frequently does), include it in the statement, especially if your client found it distressing. Some clients become very coy about telling you what was said, as though your tender ears could not cope with the whole of the story. Tell them cheerfully that they can tell you anything; you are not going to be upset, and it may be necessary for the judge to know. Write down what was said. Do not use euphemisms, even if your client does so when telling her story to you. Sometimes you may need to explain more obscure insults in the sworn statement. I had a client who was deeply affronted because she had been described as 'a Bedford Hill job'. Only local residents would have known that Bedford Hill was the local haunt of prostitutes; I thought that we could not rely on the judge knowing this, and added an explanation for why my client was so upset.

DECIDING ON YOUR COURSE OF ACTION

Once you have obtained a detailed statement from your client, consider what sort of remedy you need to use. You may be able to deal with the situation without applying to court, or you may decide to apply to court but have to choose between county court and magistrates' court proceedings.

DEALING WITH VIOLENT SITUATIONS WITHOUT INJUNCTIONS

In many cases, clients come to you asking for injunctions because they have been told to do so by the police or social workers. Sometimes you have to explain that, awful as the situation seems to her, the court will not grant her an injunction because the circumstances do not warrant one. This is not an easy message to get across, and you may have to make it quite clear that it is not you belittling what your client has been through, but the way in which the courts work.

Injunctions are not granted lightly. Not every outburst of violence in the home needs an injunction to prevent a recurrence. Very often a letter from you telling the husband to desist, and firm behaviour from your client, will work just as well, if not better. If you are only applying for a non-molestation order, the CLS will want to see that you have done this. If the circumstances merit it, you can also give the husband a deadline by which to leave the house, but this is a stronger move and probably commits you to applying for an injunction if he will not go voluntarily. It is worth bearing in mind that an injunction is a traumatic experience for *both* parties, and you should consider this carefully before you put your client through it.

At first sight a letter (such as the one at Appendix 8A) might appear to provoke rather than prevent further violence, but in general this does not prove to be the case. The advantage of it is that if there is another violent episode, the letter can be produced to the court as an exhibit to the sworn statement in support of the application for an injunction and it lends great weight to this. However, it is rare, in my experience, for this to become necessary.

Before you send such a letter you must discuss the impact it is likely to have with your client, and you can send it only if she thinks it is the best thing to do. If there is enough time, it may be helpful to send your client a draft of the letter you propose to send, so that she can assess what its likely impact will be and suggest changes if necessary. In any event, send her a copy of the final version in the same post as the letter to her husband, so that she knows what you have said and can deal with him if he accuses you of having said things which are not in the letter.

COUNTY COURT APPLICATIONS

Applications without notice to the other party (ex parte)

In the worst cases you may need to apply to the county court immediately without notice which, in practice, generally means at the beginning of the afternoon session or on the following morning. If you are going to do this, it is a good idea to phone the court first to tell them what you plan to do. This saves you arriving at court only to find that there is not a judge available, or that there is going to be such a long wait to be heard that it would have been better to apply practical rather than legal remedies.

Unless it is absolutely impossible, prepare a supporting statement, even if you have to write it out by hand. It is much easier and quicker to present the case to the court with a written statement of what has happened, and it saves putting your client in the witness box to tell her story and then finding that she becomes extremely nervous and confused.

Go to court without notice only if there really is no other way of dealing with matters. You must also fulfil the criteria of the Family Law Act 1996, s 45. The disadvantage is that you may not be able to get an order to oust the respondent immediately and, if the violence has been really serious, that is generally what is required. True, it may gain you an earlier return date than if you had made the application on notice, but this is not always so, and you may feel that the result you have achieved is rather less than anticipated. Your client may be even more disappointed because your sense of urgency has infected her, and she will not have been prepared for what she will regard as a failure if you appear to have achieved little that is concrete. If you do decide to make an application without notice you should explain the reasons, and the likely outcome, to your client carefully beforehand, so that she has a realistic idea of what you hope to achieve at the first hearing.

Do not apply without notice too often, particularly in a local court. You will quickly attract a reputation for doing so and you will start to devalue your own applications because they will not get considered entirely on their own merits. On the other hand, if you are discriminating about the applications which really are urgent, you will be taken seriously and the mere fact that you have judged it serious enough to bring to the court without notice will weigh in its favour. (The same applies to emergency funding applications, once you get known at the area office.)

Applications on notice

You will have gathered from the above that I think that this is generally the preferable way of proceeding with an application for a domestic violence injunction.

You will need to make sure that the court gives you a date far enough in advance to serve the respondent with the right period of notice, and you will need to remind your process server about this, so that if he is not successful within the required time he can let you know and you can decide what to do about the hearing.

IF YOU OBTAIN AN INJUNCTION

Make sure that your client has a copy of the order and stress to her that she should keep it safe. Take her through the various clauses so that you are sure she knows what it means. If there is a power of arrest attached, make sure the local police station has a copy and your client knows this. Advise your client that she should let you know of any attempt to breach the order as soon as possible, so that you can take further action.

RECONCILIATIONS

It is a popular myth that women who experience violence like it in some way and go back for more. If you have advised your clients sensibly and have been prudent in the use of injunctions as remedies you will find that this is not the case. Of course there will be reconciliations in some cases; it would be a poor reflection on human nature if this were not so. There will be men who are genuinely sorry and try not to repeat the behaviour, and women who have second thoughts about the course of action upon which they have embarked. In some cases a reconciliation can come about only because of what you have done to redress the balance of power in the relationship. You should not, therefore, regard what you have done as a wasted effort (nor, if your client is publicly funded, a waste of public money). In many cases injunctions work, the effects are long lasting, and a better quality of life is produced for the client.

It can be frustrating from your point of view if your client does suddenly back out. If this happens a lot, it may be time for you to review the approach you are taking to cases and to ask yourself whether you are being somewhat 'trigger-happy', dragging your clients into proceedings which they do not feel capable of sustaining. There is a particular temptation to do this if you are part of an 'injunction unit', which some firms have set up. Just because your client has been attracted by the magic power of the word 'injunction', you should not automatically assume that this is necessarily the best remedy for her.

AFTERMATH OF INJUNCTIONS

If the injunction which you have obtained was in the context of divorce proceedings this may sit uneasily with the principle of trying to approach things in a conciliatory spirit, but this should not deter you from getting your client the protection she needs if her situation is desperate. It is, however, worth bearing in mind, especially if there are children, that your client is going to have to find some way of continuing a relationship with the man against whom she has just obtained a court order. You can try to make sure that the language you use is not unduly inflammatory; you can be tough and firm without being pejorative. Do not give way to the temptation to overstate your client's case in words which may later be thrown in her face. The best approach is one which makes clear that you 'hate the sin and not the sinner'.

In cases where there are children you will have to give special consideration to suitable arrangements for contact after the injunction. In the majority of cases, the children will not have been the targets for violence, although they may have witnessed it or heard about it. There needs to be due allowance for the apprehension they may naturally feel, but at the same time it will often help if contact can be made as normal as possible. This cannot always be managed, nor is it always desirable. There is a growing recognition that children may be damaged other than physically by being close to violent relationships.

ACTING FOR THE RESPONDENT

If you do injunction work you will inevitably find that you are instructed by respondents to injunctions. Some solicitors' firms take the view that they will not act for people who are accused of domestic violence. My view, however, is that everyone should be entitled to legal representation and so I have no ethical reason for refusing to act for someone in this situation. My experience has also been that the men (and it is nearly always men) who seek representation in injunctions feel that they have a side of the story to tell, and for the most part regret what has happened – even if they are not going so far as to admit that violence is not justified. There are often reasons why domestic violence may be understandable even if it is never excusable.

It is easy to feel reasonably apprehensive about acting for someone who comes to you accused of domestic violence particularly if you are female. You may anticipate that your client is not going to be very pleased to be represented by a woman and you may be worried about the likelihood of him losing his temper with you. Try to conceal any feelings of righteous indignation about what he is accused of. Ask him to tell you his side of the story. Probably the easiest way of doing this is to go through the statement in support of the application paragraph by paragraph and line by line and find out where or whether there are material disputes about what happened. As the statement is inevitably one-sided, there will always be another side to the tale. You can then explain whether the differences add up to a material factual dispute that the court will actually take into account. It is important to phrase any comments about your client's position in an impersonal fashion, so that you explain the attitude that the judge will take, and your client understands that this is what you are doing and that you are not simply expressing your own point of view.

Unless your client actually has a mental problem which causes his violent uncontrollable behaviour you are unlikely to find that he is going to be violent or aggressive with you if you maintain a professional approach. Your own professional role protects you from this, to a large extent. And it is worth remembering that the violence exploded in a domestic context, and you, thankfully, do not have that sort of relationship together. Stay cool, calm and pleasant, and your client will respond in kind.

CHOOSING COUNSEL FOR INJUNCTIONS

Counsel for injunctions need to have particular skills. Some counsel who are very good at financial matters are not so effective when it comes to injunctions. They need to have a quality of reassurance, and even physical confidence. You should also consider the effect of the gender of the counsel whom you instruct. Sometimes it can be a good idea to instruct a woman to represent a woman, to give your client a feeling that the sisterhood is out in force. But a kind, sensible man can also be very reassuring, if only to give your client the feeling that not all men will treat her badly. I used regularly to instruct two very large male barristers for injunctions. They were both confident, kindly and courteous. They also gave the impression that if the client's husband turned nasty at court they were more than capable of sorting him out. That in itself produced its own feeling of reassurance.

FINANCIAL INJUNCTIONS

There is less to say about the technique you need to bring to bear on financial injunctions. Clearly, in many cases you need to use the without notice procedure in order to protect your client. Do consider in each case whether the circumstances warrant asking for undertakings from the other side within a specified time limit and making the application for the injunction only if these are not given.

You need to be meticulous about the facts you assert so that it is absolutely clear that you come within the scope of the powers of the court, and that the application is justified. If you do not take this trouble you may prejudice your costs.

SUMMARY

- Be prepared in advance for injunctions.
- Be thorough in the evidence you produce to the court.
- Consider carefully whether an injunction is the most appropriate remedy.
- Use without notice applications sparingly.
- Consider your choice of forum.
- Remember that there is life after injunctions for your clients.

APPENDIX 8A

SPECIMEN LETTER – PRE-INJUNCTION OR IN PLACE OF INJUNCTION

Dear Mr X

I have been consulted by [your wife] Mrs X as a result of the unhappy situation which has arisen [between you/in your marriage].

My client instructs me that over the last six months you have been violent to her on a number of occasions, the last being on [Thursday 13 March], and you have often threatened her with violence, using abusive and aggressive language to her, sometimes in the presence of the children.

I have advised my client that she is in a position to obtain an injunction against you in the Court in order to protect herself [and the children]. However, she would prefer at this stage to try to resolve things between you without the need for a Court Order, provided that you [stop your aggressive behaviour towards her immediately/take immediate steps to find somewhere else to live].

I must warn you that if, as a result of this letter, you attempt to threaten or intimidate my client in any way, or you are violent towards her, I shall have no hesitation in applying to the Court for an Order to protect her.

[My client is prepared to allow you until 12 noon on Friday 21 March to vacate her house. If you have not left by that time I have instructions to apply to the County Court for an injunction to protect my client by ordering you to leave. If it becomes necessary to apply for such an order I will ask the Court to order you to pay the costs.]

I would strongly advise you to consult solicitors of your own as soon as possible. If you do not already have a solicitor you will find that the local Citizens Advice Bureau keep a list of solicitors in your area who deal with family work. If you consult solicitors you should take this letter with you. If you do not intend to consult solicitors you may contact the writer of this letter [Miss Clout] direct by telephone.

Yours sincerely

Chapter 9

MEETINGS

Meetings can be the best possible way of advancing a case and resolving difficulties. Where the other party is represented by a solicitor whom you know and with whom you can work, you can often limit the dispute considerably. Even with a lawyer who is new to you, by the end of the meeting you may have got to know him much better so that you can deal with matters more easily in future. In family matters where you are aiming for a conciliatory approach, meetings have obvious advantages, both for discussing children and financial matters, but you should keep the two topics completely separate so that one is not traded for the other.

Meetings can also be daunting. Some lawyers use them for power games although I am not sure that in the long run this gets them anywhere. They may enjoy the feeling of control, but they probably only stiffen the resolve of the other lawyer. In matrimonial law this type of conflict between lawyers is generally unproductive.

When I was first practising, I had a case in which I was acting for a wife. At an early stage I was summoned (and I use the word advisedly) to a meeting by the husband's solicitor. She insisted that I came to her office because she was so busy and kept me waiting for 20 minutes after the time agreed. Eventually I was shown into her room. She sat behind her desk and I was put in a low chair facing her. She then proceeded to tell me how hopeless my case was and how she was not going to offer me anything. I learned a great deal from that meeting, even though in that case it got me nowhere. It taught me how meetings should not be run.

There are several books and regular seminars on meetings and the techniques of negotiation. This chapter is only intended to be a brief guide to some of the points to bear in mind. It is worth attending a few courses on the subject as they help you with technique and can be morale boosting.

DECIDING ON A MEETING

When should you suggest or agree to a meeting? The answer is when you can achieve in a meeting something which it would take longer to achieve without it. Having a meeting will sometimes shorten the number of hours lawyers have to spend on the case and thus reduce your client's costs. More often it will mean that the matter can advance at a quicker pace. For instance, you may be able to reach a settlement at an earlier date than if you had had to deal with each decision by means of post and telephone communications.

It follows that there is not much point in having a meeting unless both parties have a definite and achievable object in mind, which they both actually want to achieve. Meeting to exchange remarks and ideas may seem useful, but unless the case is advanced by the meeting it can scarcely be justified in costs.

Although the idea behind the meeting may be to avoid going to court, you should not approach it on the basis that you must reach agreement at all costs because the prospect of going to court is too awful to contemplate. Your client and the other side should be aware that if you cannot reach agreement you have the prospect of a court hearing well in mind.

AGENDAS

Agree beforehand what it is you are going to discuss. If there are a lot of items to cover, draft an agenda and agree it with the other party's legal adviser. The use of statements of issues is helpful, and solicitors are now used to setting out the differences between them in this way.

Do not try to do too much at one meeting; a limited number of points on the agenda is more helpful because the more you include the more there is to argue over. A short agenda gives greater scope for reaching an agreement.

TIMING

Avoid having a meeting too early in the case, unless all the basic matters are agreed and it is just the detail which needs tidying up. If, on the other hand, you are going to have to negotiate from first principles, you should be sure that you have had proper disclosure in advance so that you have had time to consider it thoroughly. If new and material information is produced at a meeting do not be afraid to say that you need time to consider it; if necessary, the meeting should be adjourned to give you that time.

Make sure you allow enough time for the meeting. It will almost always take longer than you think, so provide some leeway.

PLACE OF THE MEETING

The etiquette of where the meeting should take place used to be that, for the first meeting, the husband's solicitor went to the wife's solicitor's office, and this is as good a rule as any. If you have a second meeting, you can either reciprocate the hospitality of the first meeting, or continue to meet at the first venue if it was convenient.

If you are hosting the meeting, try to ensure that it is not conducted like an interview. If you sit behind your desk it suggests that you are in control of the meeting, and part of the ethic of the meeting should be that you are equals on neutral ground. Your visitor should not be made to feel the supplicant. A comfortable table with chairs around it is best, especially when the clients are present at the meeting.

BRIEFING YOUR CLIENT

If your client is going to be present at the meeting discuss it fully with her beforehand. If possible, ask your client to arrive before the meeting so that you can go through any last-minute matters together. Tell the client what to expect and establish some ground rules (no biting, no gouging, no hitting below the belt). Your client should be told what the agenda is.

PREPARING FOR THE MEETING

Make sure that you are properly briefed beforehand and that any papers you need to refer to are easily accessible. If you already know the outline of the agreement you are likely to reach, you can draft it in advance with suitable spaces left for those matters that are undecided. This saves having to look up precedents in the meeting itself.

If you are going to be negotiating major matters, you must first discuss with your client exactly what the parameters are and what the bottom line is. You should know what, in her view, are the absolutely essential things that she wants to achieve, and what are the things she would like but does not feel passionate about, so that you can afford to concede them if you have to. Such decisions will clearly have to be made in the light of any probable award by the court. If you have these things in mind, it may save the whispered taking of instructions, or having to retreat to another room to consider proposals. You cannot predict everything however. Part of the point of the meeting may be to throw up suggestions which are novel to both parties. A good negotiator should be alert to the potential for inventing options and thinking creatively. Your client may change her mind completely when she hears what is said by her husband or by his legal adviser. Do not undermine her in front of them by telling her that she is being inconsistent.

BEGINNING THE MEETING

Do not keep your visitor(s) waiting; it is ill-mannered and unprofessional and will not improve the tenor of the meeting. When you do come face to face make sure that everyone is properly introduced to everyone else. A certain formal courtesy is a good idea, especially if it is the first time you have all met each other. Do not call your client's spouse by his Christian name, unless it is made clear to you that you may.

It is helpful to have some refreshments to offer your visitors, especially through a long meeting, and can be a way to break the ice.

YOUR CLIENT'S SPOUSE

It is a good general rule to be pleasant to your client's spouse. You cannot always manage this, but it does not hurt to try. Even if your client cannot look him in the eye, your pleasantries can gradually ease matters between them. Bear in mind that your client's spouse may see you as an ogre since you are acting for the 'other side' and you may need to use all your charm to dispel this impression to achieve what you want for your client. This is particularly important when you are discussing children.

YOUR CLIENT'S FEELINGS

At the same time, be aware of your own client's feelings. Some clients will find meetings a terrible ordeal. This particularly applies to women who may not be used to 'business meetings' but whose husbands are. These women may feel at a disadvantage, and their husbands may sense this and use it to bully them. If your client is doing the bullying, you need to stop it to prevent the meeting degenerating. Alternatively, if your client is being bullied you will need to boost her morale and insist on her views being considered.

'WITHOUT PREJUDICE'

It may go without saying as far as you and the other legal adviser are concerned that the meeting is 'without prejudice', but it is worth confirming this at the beginning of the meeting, and, if you have your clients with you, you should explain to them exactly what this means. Explain also that if you reach an agreement it can be recorded and become binding.

SPARE ROOM

Try to have a spare room or space available to which people can retire if they need to discuss things privately before returning to the meeting. I have conducted a whole meeting with my client in one room and her husband and his advisers in another, as she refused to come face to face with him. This may be extreme but it worked quite well in that case.

ENDING THE MEETING

If you do reach agreement make sure that everyone feels it is absolutely right. If there is the slightest doubt, allow the clients on both sides time to think about it. If necessary, you can draw up a draft agreement and agree that for the time being it remains 'without prejudice' and that it will be sent to both clients who will consult with their lawyers within a specified time. This can reduce some of the pressure the meeting itself may have created in order to reach a settlement. In addition everyone may be so tired by the end of the meeting that their thinking may be impaired. You may also need an opportunity to work through the implications of the order – for example, the tax consequences. Clients may feel that the lawyers have conspired to achieve a settlement at any price if you try to press too much for a commitment there and then.

If you agree anything at the end of the meeting, even an agreement that you will leave certain issues unagreed for the time being, it is a good rule to record it in writing and for everyone to sign it. This saves faulty recollections at a later date. If you cannot do this in the meeting itself there should be an exchange of letters as soon as possible afterwards.

CONCLUSION

I realise that much of what I have said about meetings may be rather discouraging and give a negative impression. They are, as I have indicated, potentially dangerous, but they can be enormously useful, both for you and your client. At the end of a meeting in which agreement or understanding has been advanced, your client may feel in the happy position of being in control of what is happening in his divorce. It can restore the client to a feeling of adulthood; this is cheering and may help the relationship between the clients. A good meeting should end with a feeling that everyone has achieved something and is clearer about the way forward.

SUMMARY

- Meetings can be very useful, but there are pitfalls for the unwary.
- Agree an agenda in advance.
- Make sure your client knows what you want to achieve and you know what your client wants to achieve.
- Be civilised.
- Record agreements.

Chapter 10

RELATIONSHIP WITH COUNSEL

The purpose of this chapter is to explore why, when and how you should use counsel in a case. You also need to consider which counsel you should use.

CHOOSING COUNSEL

Good barristers work well with their instructing solicitors. Handling a case with someone you know and trust and whose judgment you respect and can rely on is enormously rewarding and productive. Ideally, you should get a real feeling of working together as a team, encouraging and stimulating each other's efforts and ideas. Gradually you get to know the people with whom such a relationship is possible, and inevitably it is to them that you will turn when the necessity for instructing counsel arises.

In the early stages of your career your choices are more curtailed. Very often you will be told which counsel to use by the partners or your more senior colleagues. You may not know who to use anyway, nor will you have the necessary experience to tell which counsel are better than others. Gradually you will gain this experience and build up a list of counsel with whom you work well. In addition, ask other colleagues in the matrimonial field to tell you who they consider competent, and make a note for future reference. If you find that counsel for the other side is impressive, add his name to your dossier. Make a note of counsel who are shown as acting in reported cases, if they appear to you to have done a good job for their clients.

After you have been practising for a while it may be tempting to use only the small number of barristers with whom you have experience, but this makes it difficult if they are all booked up when you need them and you do not know the reputation of the alternatives a clerk is offering you. It may also make it harder to match your client with the barrister who you think will best suit her.

COUNSELS' CLERKS

As you get to know a wider circle of barristers you will also get to know the quirks of their clerks. Some may, as a matter of habit, overbook their counsel so that you might not get the person you thought you were going to get. This can be frustrating for you and your clients.

Some clerks may be eternal optimists about their counsel's ability to get through paperwork. Deadlines come and go and you may never get a straight answer as to when the advice you need is going to arrive.

If you do have such difficulties with clerks, their counsel may be able to do something about it, so you should raise it with them.

WHY USE COUNSEL?

Many solicitors now do their own advocacy. If this is the policy you or your firm have taken, this part of the chapter is not meant to be an argument to make you change your mind. Rather, it is to set out the factors which, in any particular case, might induce you to use counsel at some point.

If there is going to be a hearing and you wish to have an advocate rather than present the case yourself, you will need counsel. Do not leave it to the last minute to instruct counsel. It is not really fair just to use counsel as a mouthpiece, tossing her a brief shortly before the hearing and expecting her to give it her best efforts. It is best to get counsel's input at an early stage in case it is felt that you have been running an untenable argument all the way along and that the case you want to put to the court is not one which counsel can properly put forward. It is rather like the sinking feeling you can get when you take over a file from another firm of solicitors and see that they have gone off at some tangent you would never have pursued. This will not often be the case, of course; counsel may well support your handling of the case entirely. But if you have instructed counsel at an early stage it avoids this problem and enables your client to get to know her rather than having the disconcerting experience of turning up at court with a stranger who is supposed to know all about the case.

You will also need counsel if the case requires a second opinion. You may feel that you need this because you are dealing with an area of the law with which you are unfamiliar, or which is new or controversial. You may need the backup of counsel if you have got to the point where your client is reluctant to accept the advice you have given. It can be very useful in such circumstances to say to the client that you are aware that you are not infallible and it might be a good idea to see if someone else confirms your view. Clients are familiar with the notion of the second opinion from the way doctors refer patients on to specialists, and therefore may have no difficulty understanding the rationale.

Sometimes there is the less easily defined reason that you find yourself running out of intellectual or emotional steam in a case. You feel that you cannot see a way through the problems and you have run out of ideas. When you get to this tired stage, the approach of a new mind can be extraordinarily reviving. However, you will not necessarily want to explain your reasons for involving counsel in these terms to your client or he may lose confidence in your abilities.

Some firms of solicitors use counsel as a matter of course to do most of their drafting work. They send petitions and other routine documents to counsel. This tends to be the practice of the solicitors of wealthy clients. As a matter of choice, I prefer to do most of the routine drafting myself because I enjoy it and it cuts out the delays that sending things off to counsel creates. I mention such use of counsel for the sake of completeness even though the practice is an indulgence few solicitors can make use of, and is not viable in publicly funded cases unless required as a condition of the certificate.

WHEN TO INSTRUCT COUNSEL TO ADVISE

Broadly speaking, counsel's advice will concern either law, quantum, evidence or tactics. There are three main circumstances for instructing counsel:

- at the outset of a case;
- to obtain advice during the case; or
- coming up for trial.

At the outset of the case

In some cases you will want counsel's advice, chiefly on questions of law, before the case gets properly underway. Leaving aside the practice of sending the petition to counsel to settle, there will be some cases which raise such tricky points of law that you will need to take an opinion on them before you can settle pleadings. Such cases might raise questions of jurisdiction or the finer points of nullity, such as duress. If the position is not clear from the textbooks, you will clearly need to consult counsel. In some cases, the terms of your funding certificate will mean that you have no choice but to go to counsel to take an initial opinion even if you think the law is clear on the point.

Advice during the case

In an ancillary relief case, you may wish to delay instructing counsel until you have almost completed discovery, otherwise it is difficult to have a productive conference because all counsel will do is produce a long list of things she wants you to find out. Generally, you reach an appropriate stage when Forms E have been exchanged and you are considering whether a questionnaire is apt. At this point you may want counsel to give you an indication of what she thinks on quantum; you will also need to discuss tactics. Should an offer be made at this stage? What further information do you need? What further things should be done to prepare the case for a hearing? What documents do you need to assemble to make out your client's case, or disprove her husband's assertions?

In many cases you will not consult counsel until a later stage. It may be that the case shows every likelihood of settling, but you have reached the stage where offers have been exchanged and you and your client want to be sure that the arrangements being proposed are in line with what the court would order. If the case has quirks which take it outside the usual run of your experience, or you do not have colleagues with whom you can discuss it, it can be enormously helpful to have counsel's backup at this stage.

Coming up for trial

As I have already indicated, it is a mistake to leave it to the last minute to instruct counsel if you want her to do her best for you on the day. Make sure that you fix a conference well in advance of the hearing so that you have long enough to prepare the case in the way counsel wants. I suggest three to four weeks beforehand as the ideal time. It should not be so far in advance that last-minute developments render counsel's original advice obsolete. Of course, there is the possibility that the case may settle, and then the conference may appear to have been a waste of time and resources; but it is better to be safe than sorry in this context, and it may be that your preparation for trial has been the key factor in precipitating a settlement.

HOW TO INSTRUCT COUNSEL

The preparation of instructions and briefs should be part of every solicitor's training, and the conventions are little more than applied common sense. However, my friends at the Bar tell me that generally the standard of papers they receive is very poor, so it may be helpful to give some guidance on how instructions should be done.

Every set of instructions or brief should be headed with the court heading. If there is none as yet, they should be headed 'In the matter of a proposed petition (or as appropriate) of ... (client's name)'. Beneath that, allowing enough space, you should state whether it is a brief or instructions, and what counsel is being asked to do, for example advise in conference or appear on behalf of the petitioner. You should then list the enclosures in the instructions/ brief, numbering them for easy reference. It is a matter for you how you break these up and present them for counsel to read. The main sections will usually be as follows.

Correspondence

The tradition with correspondence used to be to give counsel separate bundles, one for correspondence with the other party's legal advisers, one for that with the client, and one each for other correspondents. A number of counsel have pointed out to me that they would prefer to have it all in one continuous sequence because they find it easier to read the 'story' of the file this way. Perhaps the best thing is to ask counsel what they would like and sort the file out accordingly. Whichever way you break it up, correspondence for counsel should always be with the first letter at the top of the bundle so that it reads chronologically, and is thus the opposite way round to your file. You do not need to copy all the letters, only the ones which advance the case. Letters sent simply as reminders or acknowledgements are not generally necessary, unless, for example, you are trying to show counsel how slow someone has been to respond. As a refinement, you can stamp the copies of your letters (if they otherwise do not have your firm's letterhead on them) with a stamp with your firm's name and address to make their origin clear to counsel.

If you have edited the bundle of correspondence for counsel, it is a good idea to number it and keep a duplicate bundle for your reference, as this can save time and ambiguities if you will be referring to lots of letters in the conference. However, this does create additional photocopying, which you cannot always justify.

Pleadings

My preference is to give counsel the whole of the court documents bundle which I keep on my file (see Chapter 12). As this already has an index on the front of it, there is no need to break up the bundle with each document as a separate enclosure in the brief/instructions. Occasionally, if there is a very large document, say Form E with lots of supporting documents, and this is something on which I particularly want counsel's comments, I will put it in as a separate enclosure, but immediately behind the other pleadings so that they still run in sequence.

Other documents

If your client is publicly funded, counsel should have copies of the certificate and any amendments. The other documents you include depend on the case itself. Clearly, you will need to give counsel copies of financial documents you have had by way of disclosure. You may also want to include a proof of evidence from your client to bring counsel's attention to the background. In each case, divide the papers up into categories which should be labelled clearly and, within each category, make sure that the papers run in a chronological sequence. If there are documents missing from these sequences, such as odd bank statements, make it clear to counsel that they have not been sent to you and it is not just a mistake in the copying in your office.

If you want counsel to advise in the light of one or more cases that give a legal authority, it is sensible to copy them and include them in the instructions so as to save counsel's time and costs.

Presentation

All copies should be clear and not cut off at the sides. If they are unavoidably very faint or otherwise unreadable, explain this to counsel and try to get better copies.

All copies should be on one side of the paper only and should face the front. Backsheets on copied documents should be turned round to achieve this.

The fashion now is to send counsel's papers in ring binders with dividers to mark the enclosures. Most counsel seem to prefer this and it is certainly a tidier way of keeping all the papers together. It has the added advantage that it makes the papers much easier to update, as it is easy to take apart the ring-bound book and insert the latest correspondence and pleadings.

Contents of the instructions/brief

There are two schools of thought about the style in which you instruct counsel. One is that counsel never reads the instructions anyway and so you should just summarise everything very briefly and list the papers which you are sending and leave counsel to sort it out for himself. 'Wrap it in a back sheet and send it to counsel', they used to say. The other, which is my general view, is that you cannot expect counsel to advise properly unless he knows the whole story and the responsibility for telling the whole story is yours. This means that you must write an accurate and detailed brief. In matrimonial cases, so much of your approach to the case and to your client depends on the personality of the parties. This is not always something which counsel can glean easily from the papers in the case. Fewer and fewer clients seem to write to their solicitors with their instructions, and it is not always clear from your notes of phone calls and attendances what your client really feels, as opposed to what she wants done at any given time. It can be helpful to try to convey this to counsel, particularly if he should be warned in advance that the client is very difficult or upset.

Start the instructions by telling counsel on whose behalf he is instructed and say whether or not the client is publicly funded. Then set out the salient facts of the case, for example when the parties were married, their ages, the number of children and their names and ages. Recount what has happened so far in the proceedings and refer counsel to the particular documents in the bundle which set out the details of the case on both sides.

In most cases it is then helpful if you try to convey a sense of what the client is like, the attitude he is taking to the proceedings and the particular issue on which you want counsel to advise. If you have taken a particular attitude to an issue and advised accordingly, summarise your advice so far. Counsel may support what you have done so far, or may feel that your position is not tenable or there are certain points which you have not stressed which should be emphasised to the client. It helps counsel if he knows at the outset what attitude you have been taking so that he can tell whether his opinion is going to come as a shock to the client or whether you have already prepared the ground.

At the end of the instructions, you should list clearly the points on which you want counsel to advise. It helps if you number these and set them out. For instance:

'Counsel is therefore asked to advise on the following:

1. Whether the *Calderbank* offer should be accepted.
2. If not, what award he feels a court would be likely to make.
3. Whether further discovery should be sought from the respondent, and, if appropriate, to settle a questionnaire.
4. What further evidence should be produced by the petitioner.
5. Generally.'

It is always a good idea to ask for general advice at the end. Briefs should end more simply: by requesting counsel to attend court for your client and seek to obtain the order you want.

At the very end of the instructions/brief, put your initials and date. This helps you to sort out papers on the file later on, when it is not always clear in which order documents were produced. It also helps you if you have subsequently to update the papers, as it is easy for you to check the date from which you need to start adding recent material.

SENDING THE PAPERS TO COUNSEL

Make sure that counsel has the papers in good time if you are going to see her in conference. It is not fair, or very realistic, to expect counsel to have assimilated everything overnight. If the case is very complex, warn counsel's clerk in advance so that he can pass the message on and your counsel can leave enough time to get to grips with the issues.

If you want a document settled urgently, attach a little note to the instructions pointing this out and requesting counsel's speedy attention.

AGREEING A FEE

Many solicitors have difficulty agreeing counsel's fees, often from embarrassment. Some clerks are aware of this diffidence and may use it to their advantage to avoid negotiation. I was trained to believe that you never agreed what was first asked and always named a lower figure, but I have not always kept to this rule. It depends on the clerk and the counsel you are using, and the sort of budget you know your client has available. This is one area where you will need to ask your colleagues for advice. Do be positive in your approach, however, and try to conquer the reticence that seems to sweep over the profession when the subject of money is raised.

It is especially important to agree a fee for a brief because of the higher amounts involved, particularly if the hearing is likely to be lengthy. It is therefore good practice to mark the agreed fee on the papers you send to counsel.

In a publicly funded case, the papers should be marked boldly with the words 'Public Funding'. The issue of the fee can be left to the clerk who will have an idea of what he can obtain on taxation.

NASTY HABITS

Much of one's relationship with counsel is good and productive, but there may be problems which should be aired, and under which it is easy to be cowed when you are fairly new to the game. I intend to air some of them now.

Do not let counsel bully you or the client. Being the instructing solicitor means what it says; you give the instructions. You can change counsel, in mid-case if you have to, and although it is not a step to be undertaken lightly, it is an option you should consider if you feel that counsel is not following your instructions or is being offensive to you or to the client. After all, the ultimate responsibility is yours.

A few counsel have a nasty habit of taking a very aggressive, bullish approach on cases up to the last minute, when the briefs have been delivered and you are all outside the court door. They then advise settlement, and the figures they had been advising are suddenly reduced. If your counsel advises your client that higher figures than you think are realistic may be obtained and seldom achieves those figures at hearings, you should consider whether it is a good idea to continue to instruct him.

SUMMARY

- Choose counsel as part of a team.
- Get to know the counsels' clerks.
- Counsel are useful for second opinions, for casting a fresh eye over the case when you are jaded, and for some types of drafting.
- Consider carefully the timing of instructing counsel.
- Take pains with counsel's bundle.
- Tell counsel the whole story.
- Do not put up with unhelpful behaviour from counsel or clerks.

Chapter 11

GOING TO COURT

The two situations in which you are most likely to find yourself going to court could hardly be more different. Emergency injunctions may require you to rush off with all the preparation having to be done at speed, while contested applications about money or children will usually have had weeks or months of preparation for a fixed date. I have already dealt in other chapters with the things that you need to do for the different types of applications; the purpose of this chapter is to set out some general rules about going to court that apply whatever the reason for your being there.

Going to court can be an experience fraught with anxiety because it has an all-or-nothing feel. Generally, you will not have another opportunity to put your client's case. To some extent your role becomes that of the stage manager (unless you are doing your own advocacy, in which case you have a speaking part as well). You have to co-ordinate everyone's efforts and make sure that everyone gets there on time, with all necessary papers and props available.

WHAT TO TELL THE CLIENT

Make sure you brief your client before the hearing so that she knows what to expect. You cannot prevent her from feeling nervous, but you can minimise some of the natural worries she will inevitably have, and this will help her to concentrate on the hearing itself. Accordingly, it makes sense to advise your client on the following points.

- *What to wear.* You will know the effect you want to achieve. Generally, this means tidy and respectable and not too flashy.
- *Where to meet you.* Decide whether it is best to meet at court or elsewhere. Describe how to get there clearly to the client. In some cases, provide a map.
- *What to expect.*
  - Describe the room in which the hearing will take place. Many clients are taken aback when they see what a district judge's room is like, and realise that they have to sit opposite their spouses.

- Warn the client about how long it is likely to take and, if appropriate, warn about the hanging around that has to be endured. Suggest that your client brings something to read or do to while away the time. One of my clients once crocheted the larger part of a baby's shawl as we waited for an injunction.
- Tell the client the order in which the case takes place, ie examination, cross-examination, re-examination, speeches and judgment, etc, so that she gets an idea of what is going on and what will happen next. Explain that the hearing is in private, and friends will have to sit outside.
- Explain technical terms which may crop up. One of my clients thought that 'in camera' meant that the case was to be filmed.

Do not underestimate what an ordeal it will be for your client. If you feel nervous, she may be feeling ten times worse. Allow for this in the way you deal with her, and warn her that this is likely to happen, but that it is a natural reaction. Tell her that it will be over sooner than she thinks; once you are in court the time seems to go faster, the way it does in exams; you are too busy to be very nervous.

PAPERS FOR COURT

Practice Direction (Family Proceedings: Court Bundles) of 20 March 2000 [2000] 1 FLR 536 deals with the preparation of bundles, which you must observe. You should do more than just observe the letter of the law, which says:

> 'Bundles should be paginated and indexed and should contain all and only relevant documents in chronological order within separate sections for applications and orders; statements and affidavits; expert and other other reports; and miscellaneous documents. Bundles should be agreed, if possible, and should include a summary, a statement of issues, a chronology and skeleton arguments together with copies of all authorities to be cited. The bundles should be clearly marked with the case title and number and the judge's name, if known, and should be lodged two clear days prior to the hearing.'

Make sure that the bundles look tidy, with matching colours for the covers, neat index cards and clear tabulation. You will get enormous approval from the court if everything looks professional and, while it may not influence the judge to look benevolently on your client, it can do not harm. If the papers look messy and the judge is annoyed, your client may feel that this has contributed to a decision which has gone against him.

Preparing bundles

The convention is, generally, that the applicant's adviser prepares the bundles for court. However, if you are the respondent to the application, you cannot always rely on the other adviser to do this, and you should check well in advance whether he has it in hand. If not, or you have had a bad experience with that solicitor in the past, it is probably better to do it yourself. The worst situation is where a mass of unlabelled, undivided paper arrives only a day or two before the hearing, or where nothing gets agreed and you arrive at court with a loose handful each.

What goes in the bundles

The Practice Direction gives you an outline only as to what should go in the bundles, and generally you have to use your common sense. Bundles are prepared so that you have at court, in an easily located form, all the documentary evidence on which either party intends to rely.

If you are using counsel, you should check with him what documents he particularly intends to rely on, and these should definitely be included. You should also check with the other party's lawyer, as bundles should be agreed if possible, by writing him a formal letter to ask what he wants included. If your selections differ, you should tell him what other documents you want included. If you do this properly, you can narrow down the issues between the parties. Where matters are agreed (such as valuations), it is only necessary to include those documents the judge may want to see for background. You should also consult counsel about the summary, statement of issues, chronology and skeleton arguments.

Inevitably, you will have to copy the original documents for the bundles. Sometimes a query is raised about the copy, because it is too faint or edges have been cut off, or the authenticity of the copy is in question. To avoid such controversies it is a good idea to have one bundle which has all the originals in it; this is the copy I prefer to retain. It will look untidier than the photocopied version, and it is probably better to let the judge have the tidier one. If you give it to counsel he may want to write his own notes all over it. For obvious reasons, you will not want to hand this bundle over to the other lawyer.

Keep the bundle as small as you can. Do not pad it out with unnecessary documents, such as correspondence between solicitors which no one will need to see. Apart from any other consideration, a small bundle saves on photocopying.

When you consider what documents should be in the bundle, bear in mind the Practice Direction above, but do not confine yourself merely to what has been generated by the case. Be creative. Think about the evidence you need to establish your case. If rehousing either party is an issue, obtain recent estate agents' particulars to show the spread of property prices in suitable areas. The advertising freesheets distributed in local areas are useful for this as they usually have pages with lots of photographs of properties which can easily be compared. If it seems likely that a question relating to the area will be raised, you cannot rely on the judge being familiar with the locality. Get a map or two and find out about local transport. If job opportunities are an issue, get hold of the local paper and look at the availability of suitable work, or enquire at the Jobcentre, to see what opportunities exist. This is your chance to play detective. In some cases your client will do it himself, either spontaneously or at your prompting, but sometimes you have to do it yourself to make sure that it is done properly.

Arranging the bundles

Presentation, as I have stressed elsewhere, is enormously important. Sort the documents as stipulated by the Practice Direction cited above. Provide an index to the bundle and make liberal use of dividers so that documents are easily located. In the absence of dividers use stick-on tags written legibly. In each division, page the documents and make sure that the bundles are all the same; your index should give the page numbers. Use different colours and markers to make items clear and distinctive. If your firm has a logo, or labels printed with its name, you can use these to make the bundles look smart. The higher the court, the more attention you will need to give to getting everything right.

How many bundles?

Four is the minimum number of bundles required at first instance; the number is sometimes specified in the directions of the court. This gives you one for your counsel, one for the judge, one for the other party's adviser (from which he makes his own copies), and one for you. However, another bundle is sometimes useful because a witness may need to refer to it; if you do not have a spare you will have to pass him yours, in which case you cannot see what is being referred to by counsel and the witness. If the Forms E and questionnaires have not been included in the bundle, have a spare set ready for this purpose, and page and index that bundle, because otherwise locating documents may take a frustrating length of time. In higher courts you will need extra bundles, one for each judge and others for extra counsel if you use them. The House of Lords has its own rules. On every appeal, check the latest rules as these can change without your noticing them.

TAKING A NOTE

Taking notes can be the worst part of being the instructing solicitor in a case. You can get awful writer's cramp. It can be difficult to know what exactly to record because everyone seems to have their own way of doing it and there is little guidance. The following seem to be sensible tips which I have gleaned over the years.

- Use a notebook stapled at the side, such as a counsel's notebook, rather than one fastened at the top, since there is never enough depth to the table to allow for flipping the pages over.
- Write on one side of the paper only. When you get to the end of the book, turn it upside down and go back on the clean sides.
- Mentally divide your page into two columns and write questions on the left and answers on the right.
- Abbreviate where you can. 'Yes' and 'No' become Y and N, but do not use shorthand which cannot be understood by someone else because counsel may well want to refer to your book to check what was said.
- Have a good supply of pens so that you do not run out.
- If you need to take up a point with counsel, write a clear note and pass it to her.
- Where a witness is being examined on a document, make sure that your note clearly identifies which one is concerned. It helps if you have paged the bundle because you can refer simply to the page numbers. Where there are specific parts of documents, such as entries on bank statements, about which there are questions, you can mark your bundle, identifying each item with a number in a circle or a letter and recording that number in your notes so that you can locate them easily later if you need to.
- Above all, take pains to get as detailed a verbatim note of the judgment as you possibly can because you will need to produce this if there is an appeal. *You can never be sure in advance that this is something which will not happen.* You will also need to check that the order which you eventually get from the court is the same as your note of what the judge ordered.

OTHER EQUIPMENT TO TAKE TO COURT

It is a good idea, in addition to all the legal paraphernalia, to carry with you other items which may be useful – most of which can lurk in your briefcase in case you ever need them. For example:

- cigarettes (if you smoke), peppermints and coughdrops;
- a clean handkerchief or tissues – for you and for the upset client;
- a crossword and something to read – or to offer to the client to read; if children are going to attend, a magazine or small puzzle is very useful and your client may well be too fraught to have thought of this;
- Tippex and a stapler in case you have to write out an order;

- a calculator – essential for following the judge's sums, and often forgotten by counsel;
- notebook(s), a supply of pens and/or ink and bookstraps, for bundling up all the papers;
- change (plenty of it) for the phone/coffee machine and phonecards or a mobile phone;
- one more copy of any material document than you thought you needed.

YOUR MANNER AT COURT

On the day of the hearing you will have to play a supportive role. You need to encourage and reassure your client. A fund of legal stories and jokes may come in useful. Part of your role is hand-holding, in the metaphorical sense, and in some cases physical contact from you, a held hand or a hug, may also be appropriate.

If you have a long wait, use it to run through once more with your client what will happen when you go into court. Resist the temptation to 'coach' the testimony; if it comes out too pat in court it is likely to sound false. Remind your client that the advocate does the talking in court and she should not say things out of turn. Remind her to answer the question and not what she perceives to be the motive behind it. If you think she is likely to be a good witness tell her this as it is morale boosting. If this is not the case, do not undermine her just before the hearing by pointing it out; instead, give her some tips towards improving her performance.

Make sure your client knows what is going on. Counsel have a tendency to scurry away in corners to have long private chats, and it is possible that your client may feel excluded and caught up in a process over which she has no control. If there are discussions about settlement, you need to ensure that undue pressure is not brought to bear on her, and that anything she agrees to is fully understood by her. Clients often complain later that they did not know what was happening or what the effects of the settlement would be.

Everyone likes to settle cases, but there are some cases in which the desperate quest for settlement outside court is not worth it. Beware of counsel who lose heart and press for a quick settlement rather than a prolonged hearing. Where the client has attended the hearing, it would be better if the matter was heard; after so much emotion and effort, a hasty settlement can be a sad let-down. In some cases the opportunity to put the dispute before an independent arbitrator may have its own cathartic contribution to make to your client's life.

AFTER THE HEARING

When you come out of court take the time to explain to your client what has happened. He will have found it difficult to pick out the 'meat' from the judgment and may have got completely lost, particularly in the discussion on costs at the end of the hearing. Go through the order with him and, if necessary, jot it down for him so that he can take a note of it away with him. If immediate action on his part is required, such as payment of an instalment of maintenance, make sure he knows what he has to do and by what date. Explain the effect of orders on costs and any other technical matters which may not be self-explanatory.

If you have 'lost' (unlike other litigation, it is not always obvious whether or not you have), express your regrets. You can do this without any suggestion being made that you have not handled the case properly. If your client needs a post-mortem, you will probably need to arrange a further appointment unless there is somewhere at the court where you can sit down privately so that you can go through things properly. Your counsel, if you have one, should do this with you. If there is the possibility of an appeal you need to discuss this, and quickly, because the time limits are quite tight.

Even if you have 'won' it is probably worthwhile warning your client that there is generally a feeling of anticlimax after the hearing. He may need to take a little time to get used to life without litigation. You may also be affected and may well feel completely worn out afterwards and take a few days to get back to normal. If you know that this is likely to happen, you can allow for it and it is less disconcerting.

WHEN YOU GET THE ORDER

Check the wording carefully against your note of the order made at the time. If there is a discrepancy, check with counsel (if appropriate) and the other solicitor. If they agree that it is wrong you can apply for an amendment to be made under the 'slip rule'. If you cannot agree as to what the order should say you will have to take the matter up with the judge and see what he has noted down in his notebook.

SUMMARY

- Prepare the client properly.
- Make sure that the papers are in good order.
- Take a detailed note.
- Take useful equipment.

- Be supportive to your client.
- Never apply undue pressure to your client to achieve a settlement.
- Explain what happened afterwards.
- Check the order.

Chapter 12

KEEPING THE FILE

Files should be kept in such a way that if anyone else works on them it is possible to find out easily what is happening on each one. In order to achieve this, you have to do two things: you must keep the file up to date; and keep the documents in a recognisable order so that they are easy to find.

This is not mere pedantry; it is a rule of survival for the litigation lawyer. In my experience it is the only way to deal efficiently with large volumes of litigation, particularly if most of your work is publicly funded. Unless you impose some sort of system, deadlines get missed and papers get lost. If you are delegating routine matters (as you frequently have to with publicly funded cases in order to make them profitable) it makes life easier for you and your colleagues if you have a system and you all stick to it so that you all know what to expect to find on each file.

Further, franchising criteria impose their own structures on file keeping that you have to observe.

A SYSTEM FOR THE FILE

This chapter sets out the system I have adopted, after many years of trial and error. It is not the only way to keep a file, but it may give you some ideas for your own way of working. What is important is that you have a system which works well and, if possible, is used by everyone in your department so that you have continuity if the file changes hands. It saves everyone's time in the long run, and saving time makes you money.

Whatever system you use make sure that everyone, particularly your secretary, knows what it is and keeps to it. It may seem like a chore at first, but once it becomes familiar it is reduced to habit and takes everyone less time.

In my system, each case file has two sections: one for correspondence and attendances and one for documents. I prefer to keep the documents in an envelope-type file so that it keeps the papers safe. If additional files are used the main file indicates their existence. For instance, I write 'Court Documents in red ring binder' on the front cover or stick labels on with 'File 1 of 3', 'File 2 of 3', etc, to remind me, and my colleagues, of the existence of the others.

FLYLEAF

It is useful to record some basic information on the cover of the file itself, so that you do not have to look it up each time. You can devise a form which you can run off on the photocopier or computer and stick on each file (see Appendix 12A).

CORRESPONDENCE BUNDLE

All correspondence and attendance notes are filed on one bundle in chronological order, with the most recent uppermost. All attendances, and the time spent on them, are noted, if possible by dictated notes, but otherwise by legible written ones. Perusals and other time spent on the file are recorded on this bundle (see Chapter 13).

A checklist of the steps in the proceedings attached to the file, which you fill in as you proceed, can be useful in keeping you alert to time limits or lapses of time.

DIVIDING UP THE DOCUMENTS

All documents other than correspondence and file notes are kept in the second section. It is best if they are further divided and this can be easily and cheaply done by using folded A3 sheets which are clearly marked. You can keep the following labelled in large letters and ready photocopied:

- drafts;
- disbursements/bills;
- spare copies;
- counsel's papers;
- court documents.

Drafts

Drafts are kept in a separate section and dated. If they are sent out for approval, the date on which this is done is marked on them on the front. It helps if they are filed on a split pin or tag so that they stay in order, with the most recent uppermost. This identifies the version is being dealt with at any given time. This is particularly useful when someone phones to discuss a draft. It makes sense to keep only one copy of each draft in this folder to avoid confusion over the version you are working on.

Disbursements and bills

This folder contains all counsel's fee notes and bills from others such as enquiry agents and surveyors. It makes it easier for the costs draughtsman to find them at the end of the case, so it is particularly important in publicly funded cases, but it also makes drawing a private client bill easier. Interim bills can also be kept there.

Spare copies

It is confusing if there is more than one copy of a document on the file. Spare copies can be kept in a separate folder, which can be plundered to make up counsel's brief and save on photocopying.

Counsel's papers

In this section I keep a copy of all briefs, instructions and notes to counsel. Each one is marked with the date on which it was prepared and sent to counsel and, if possible, they are kept in date order with the most recent on top. (It is best practice, if you have prepared for counsel an edited bundle of, say, correspondence, to keep a duplicate with the same paging, but time and resources do not always permit this.)

Court documents

In addition, I keep a court documents bundle with a front index sheet (see Appendix 12B) which is added to with each document, identified by its description and date. I use the term 'court documents' loosely in this context to connote all documents (not letters) which are filed at the court. I generally also file the CLS applications, certificates and amendments on this bundle, but you can have a separate folder for these if you prefer. My fact file is always the first document on this bundle, even though it is not a 'court' document, as it gives anyone a résumé of the case in concise form. This is particularly useful for counsel, to whom the whole bundle can be copied. When the bundle starts to get about half an inch thick, it is useful to start paging the bundle and, thereafter, as documents are added, to keep the paging up to date. When the bundle gets really thick, about one inch, I transfer it to a ring binder so that the papers are easily retrieved and do not get too dog-eared.

Only completed documents, for example statements that have been sworn, with the jurat completed, are put on the court documents bundle. Only one copy of each document goes on the bundle. All documents are on one side of the paper only and face forwards. This means that back sheets are turned round to face forwards. All staples should be taken out so that photocopying for counsel can be achieved quickly, and reference to the text of the documents is more accessible.

Manuscript notes

Long, handwritten notes of attendances, such as personal interviews with the client, are dictated in a coherent form and put on the correspondence bundle so that another colleague referring to the file can see what has happened. Handwritten notes can therefore be kept in a separate bundle on the file. They are invaluable as primary source material and should not be disposed of even when they have been transcribed.

If it appears that a case is going to require a number of attendances at court, personal attendances on the client, or conferences with counsel, I find it is good practice at the outset to take a separate notebook and keep this for all handwritten notes so that they are kept in a tidy and chronological order. The notebook is clearly labelled on the front with the case to which it refers, and the office file number, just in case it ever becomes detached from the main file. Subsequently, if it seems helpful, I page and index the notebook on the front cover.

Original documents

Original and important documents such as a marriage certificate must be kept safely. Plastic folders are useful for this. Precious small originals such as photographs can be put in envelopes and stapled to the file.

NOTING COMMENTS ON DOCUMENTS

If I go through a document on the file with a client and need comments on the documents I do not use the copy on the court documents bundle, but take another for this purpose, so that one copy is unmarked in case I need to copy it again. For similar reasons, you should only ever write comments on an original letter in pencil.

FILING

The obvious corollary of any system like this is that the filing has to be kept up to date. I once ran a very successful system where I put anything which needed filing into a basket and first thing next morning my secretary would spend some time filing it as we talked through what we were going to do that day. At the next office I moved to, my secretary was wholly resistant to the suggestion and it got done in batches when she felt like it. In some cases it is probably better to do it yourself, if you can make sure that you do it regularly.

SUMMARY

- Colleagues should be able to pick up your file and know what is happening.
- Devise a system of keeping your files in order.
- Make sure your secretary and your colleagues know your system.
- Keep your filing up to date.

APPENDIX 12A

FLY LEAF SHEET

CLIENT	
NAME	
ADDRESS	
TEL: HOME	
TEL: WORK	

SOLICITORS FOR SPOUSE	
NAME	
ADDRESS	
DX	
REF	
TEL	
FAX	

COURT	
TITLE NO	
TEL	
FAX	

CLS FUNDING NO	

COUNSEL	
CHAMBERS	
TEL	
FAX	

OTHER USEFUL INFORMATION

APPENDIX 12B

COURT DOCUMENTS BUNDLE FRONT SHEET

Court:
Title No.

Page	Document	Date

Chapter 13

COSTS

Some solicitors (particularly those who are committed to publicly funded work) seem to think that it is wrong to have profit-making as one of the aims of professional life. I agree, if making a profit becomes the sole aim of your practice with the result that clients and staff are sacrificed to it. However, it is possible to combine the two aims of making a profit and providing a proper service for your client. Indeed, you will provide a better service if you are able to run it professionally and efficiently so as to make money at it.

The key to this is dealing with costs efficiently and the way to do that is by systematic time recording. This holds true both for private and public work and so I will deal with it before I go on to the particular techniques you can employ for each of those two sorts of work.

TIME RECORDING

In all publicly funded cases and in cases where your costs are disputed either by your client or by her spouse's solicitors (where you have an order for your costs to be paid by him), you are paid according to the work recorded on the file. A computer printout, if you have one, is of little if any help unless it is backed up with notes on the file.

Most firms now use a central computer to record time; a time-sheet is completed either by hand or on screen each week and these are collated centrally to produce a printout of time and therefore costs on each file. In most private cases, this is all that is required, as a bill drawn up in this way will generally be paid by the client. However, you cannot predict what the likely outcome on costs in each case will be, so everything you do should be recorded on the file with a note of the time it took. Most firms have some sort of attendance pad, if only for recording phone calls and this can be adapted to include all other sorts of work. Alternatively, you can devise your own attendance sheet, which you can run off on the photocopier or print from the computer (see Appendix 13A).

Clearly, phone calls must be recorded, but remember to include your time spent reading the file and drafting. If you have spent more than routine time reading incoming letters, for example because they are very long or contain documents you need to study, make a note of the time you spend on them. With handwritten drafts, it is a useful technique to note on the top of the first page the time you start and then write in the finishing time at the end.

It may be difficult to put all these procedures into practice at first, but one answer is to keep going doggedly until they become a matter of habit. Even then, a crisis, or several telephone calls and other interruptions in a morning, can make you lose all track of the time you have spent. I have found it very useful to have a small digital clock which sits in my pencil tray and is a very visible reminder of the time (one of my colleagues uses the municipal clock tower outside the window); it is easier than remembering to look at my watch and quicker to read. It is now a habit to note the time a telephone call starts and when it finishes; for long telephone calls this is particularly useful because I always tend to underestimate the time I have spent on the phone.

PRIVATE CLIENT

Some clients have a strange attitude towards costs. They do not think that solicitors need paying, and consider that it is acceptable to leave bills unpaid for weeks, months, or even years. I once had a client who did not qualify for Green Form legal advice (as it then was); when I told her that she would have to pay privately she said in a tone of outrage, 'What? Pay? For advice?'. With some clients it may be helpful to draw the analogy that they would not walk round Sainsburys and fill up a trolley and walk out without paying. (If your client also has a criminal record for offences of dishonesty, this may not be the most helpful analogy.)

Most clients will ask what you charge, and may even want this information from you when they ring up to make the first appointment, but some forget or seem to behave as if they would rather not know. They may think it is vulgar to discuss such matters, or are too embarrassed (or scared) to ask, but you should tell them anyway. It is now a requirement of The Law Society and it saves arguments later. As well as telling clients in the first interview, you should write to confirm the position on costs in a separate 'client care' letter. This protects you if your basis of charging is later questioned, and can protect you if you are obliged to have your bill assessed.

Your firm will probably have a standard 'client care' letter which you are expected to use. Read it through carefully and think about whether it is going to be clear to your clients. Your explanation of the basis of costs should be unambiguous. State your hourly rate; if there is uplift, say so, and explain how it works. Emphasise that VAT and disbursements are not included. For some clients you may have to explain the word 'disbursements'.

Money on account

Most firms will want you to take money on account of future costs. Do not be afraid to name a realistic figure. The proportion and amount must be a matter of individual policy. Sometimes clients do not have large sums put by which they can pay over to you. My experience has been that they are often happy to pay a regular amount each month, and you can assist them with this either by taking a set of post-dated cheques which you keep safely on the file and pay in each month, or by asking your accounts department to provide you with a standard form of standing order. You can ask your client to complete this at the first interview.

Keeping costs in check

If you have a central time recording system, keeping check on costs is done for you. You can call for an up-to-date printout or display on screen whenever you need to and see what costs have been incurred. If it seems appropriate, you can then render a bill immediately. Without such a system you are, at any given point, blind to the state of costs on the file. (The time-honoured solicitor's method of feeling the weight of the file is no longer acceptable.) Costs can get out of hand, and by the time you get round to rendering a bill to the client or the CLS, you get a howl of protest from the client who might have been perfectly happy with a sequence of smaller bills.

One way of preventing this, in the absence of automatic systems, is to keep a running costs sheet in the front of each file, such as I suggest for public funding cases below (see Appendix 13B). Every time you get the file out for work you can complete this and either add up the total as you go or do so once a month. This means that if the client asks for a spot check on costs you can respond virtually immediately. It saves time when it comes to billing as you do not have to run back through the file doing a costing each time, a task which I used to find so cripplingly boring that I would do anything to put it off.

Regular bills

Some private clients specifically ask for regular bills, which can be a good idea, although the administrative effort becomes onerous if they are monthly. Billing every two months or every quarter works quite well. You need to consider what the firm's policy is going to be if these bills are not paid. How long will you continue to work on the file?

One problem with sending bills out at regular times is that the flow of work in a matrimonial case is not even. You do a great deal when you first take instructions and a good deal at the end when you have a settlement or a final hearing, but in between there are lulls punctuated with bursts of activity. This means that the level of billing can fluctuate for reasons which are not obvious to your client. You should explain at the outset that this may happen, rather then letting it lead to misunderstandings later.

Funding the case

If your firm does not accept public funding cases and you are approached by a client who does not have much money of her own at the outset of the case, but who will have a sufficient settlement at the end of the case if it goes as it should, you can agree to act on the basis that you will be paid when the client comes into funds. This is not taking a contingency fee, because the payment is not conditional on the result of the case, and it is a proper method of proceeding. Some firms have a policy of doing this. The arrangement has received judicial approval, subject to safeguards (*Sears Tooth (a firm) v Payne Hicks Beach (a firm)* [1997] 2 FLR 116). Some firms require their clients to borrow the money to pay them on account against their future prospects, and there are a number of bank managers who will lend on this basis.

Such arrangements should be handled with the greatest of care. Often a bank will want a letter from you to back up the client's application for a loan; or the bank may want an undertaking from you to remit the account your client receives in settlement to the bank. You cannot write such a letter unless you are absolutely certain that the money will be available at the end of the case to cover the loan, and in many cases one party to the marriage will have only the haziest knowledge of what the other is really worth. Also, you cannot always be sure that the money will come through your hands. In many cases it comes from the sale of a house and that sale is handled by another firm of solicitors. Nor can you always be certain when the money will be available. The property market is moving rapidly at the time of writing, but this has not always been the case. The interest on loans taken out in anticipation of such sales will mount up. Beware, therefore, of how you phrase such a letter, lest you trap yourself into giving an irrevocable undertaking which you may be powerless to fulfil. Most firms will insist that any undertaking you give is checked with a senior person in the department or the firm in any event.

If the client will probably qualify for public funding, but this is not something your firm offers, you should explain this to her. Of course, you can point out that even with public funding the client is going to pay towards her costs because of the operation of the statutory charge, but public funding may still work out cheaper for her; your firm may be charging your time out at far more per hour than you would get paid after a CLS assessment. It is wrong to deny your client the knowledge which would enable her to make an informed decision on the matter.

Rendering the bill

American lawyers say: 'bill them while the tears are falling'. Put the bill in soon after you have completed a piece of work or the case itself; gratitude from your client fades fast – a natural human reaction. You can even put in your bill before all work is completed, if, for example, you are just waiting to get the decree absolute from the court, and express the bill (and cost it) to include the work of sending the final papers to the client. In some cases you may feel it prudent to retain your lien on those papers until your bill is paid.

PUBLIC FUNDING

It is difficult to make publicly funded work profitable, but it can be done. The key factors are efficiency and volume. The more publicly funded work you do, the better you will be at the routine administrative things it involves and for which you do not get paid. Unless, you are used to, for example, sending off a costs claim form, it can take you ages. Volume is not necessarily something over which you have much control, but efficiency is.

Public funding applications

Applications for public funding should be made as soon as possible. Get your client to sign all the necessary forms at the first interview. If your client will have to attend a mediation, make the appointment while she is with you.

There is no need for you to complete the forms personally. This is something which can often be delegated to your secretary or an assistant who can be taught how to complete them. If you have a standard letter which can accompany the forms to the CLS office, the task is quickly done without you having to spend extra time over it.

Given the delays in granting of funding, it makes sense to send the forms off immediately. The quicker you get a full certificate, the quicker you will be paid at higher rates than Legal Help and the quicker you can get on with your client's case.

Standard letters

Computers enable you to present your standard letters in a professional way. The time spent setting up standard letters pays off in terms of costs. Set up as many as you possibly can. All routine matters, such as sending the petition to the court or sending the client her decree absolute, can be dealt with in a standard letter with spaces for inserting individual client's details such as name, address, dates, etc.

Legal Help extensions

Unless you get into a routine for applying for Legal Help extensions, they can take up more time than you can justify in the way of costs. It saves a lot of time if you keep a running note of costs inside the file in the same way as I have suggested you do for private client work (see Appendix 13B). Keeping this up to date can become second nature, and you can quickly spot when an extension will be necessary.

Recording bills delivered

Your firm will have a central procedure for recording bills submitted, but, I suggest that you keep your own list of the bills, both private client and public funding, that you submit so that you can chase up unpaid ones. You can rule a notebook up as follows:

Client name	Type of bill	Date sent	Costs	VAT	Disbursements plus VAT	Date paid

If you keep this record with a new page for each month, you can see at a glance the unpaid bills that need chasing up. A standard letter is also useful here. All this helps to make the task of administering costs more efficient, quicker and much less boring for you.

SUMMARY

- If you do it, record it.
- Be straightforward about costs with your clients.
- Be aware of the level of costs on the file.
- Bill regularly where you can.
- Streamline your public funding work.

APPENDIX 13A

TIME-RECORDING SHEET

Client	Date	
Matter		
Work done	Time spent	Time begun
telephone call out		
in		Time ended
personal attendance		
drafting		
perusing		
court attendance		
conference with counsel		
travelling time		

General notes

APPENDIX 13B

RUNNING TOTAL COSTS SHEET

DATE	TIME TAKEN	WORK DONE							RUNNING TOTAL
		Tick				Give details below			
		L/I	L/O	T/A In	T/A Out	Personal Attendance	Drafting	Perusals	

APPENDIX 13C

LEGAL HELP COSTS CHECK

WORK TYPE				DATE	TIME SPENT	COST £	RUNNING TOTAL £
Disbs	P.A.	T.A.	L.O.				
		·					

DATE OF COSTING	EXTENSION ASKED	DATE	AMOUNT GRANTED

Chapter 14

GETTING CLIENTS: PUBLICITY AND IMAGE

If you are employed by a firm which already has a considerable reputation for matrimonial work in your community, or even one which has its publicity handled by an agency, this chapter is not for you. However, some firms do not bother about publicity; they probably do not advertise in any organised way and have no 'house style' other than the logo on their letterheads. If you are in this situation, there is great potential to consider what publicity you want, if any, and what form it should take.

WHY BOTHER?

Why should you think about what sort of image you have and where your clients come from? Because, although there is a lot of family work around and it is not quite as dependent on market forces as conveyancing, there are also a lot of good matrimonial lawyers practising in this field and you need to make sure that you are one of them and continue to build up your practice. If you are good, why shouldn't it be known so that more clients can benefit from your good service?

Unfortunately, you cannot rely on the fact that you are good to bring in the work. It may bring some in because matrimonial clients tend to pass on your name, and people who need family lawyers ask around among their friends to find someone sympathetic. You will acquire clients this way, but it is a long-term process which will take years to build up. We are encouraged as a profession to seek new clients actively. Take advantage of this.

MAKING CONTACTS

There are other sources of work, some of which you can exploit personally. Several agencies are asked by potential clients to recommend solicitors, for example Citizens Advice Bureaux, social services, women's refuges, local help agencies, the local courts, and other firms of solicitors which do not handle family work. Build up your contacts with these agencies; make yourself known to them.

You could consider putting up posters in the offices of these other agencies (where appropriate), or leaving a brochure from your firm. You could also meet the people who run these offices and make contact in this way. Most important, however, is the way in which you react if they ring you up to send you a client. You need to be demonstrably helpful and prompt in your response. This will ensure that they continue to send you work. If you do not appear to be keen and responsive, you will not be the first person they think of when they next get an enquiry.

Get to know the other local legal advisers who practise in your field. There will be a regional branch of the Solicitors Family Law Association that you can join. In some cases you may need to pass clients on to other practitioners; if you do, ask the client to mention that you sent him. The compliment may well be returned in due course.

ADVERTISING

If you decide to have an advertising campaign, make sure you have the capacity to deal with the increased work it will generate, otherwise you will have to turn eager clients away, which is self-defeating. It is no use advertising if you are already over-worked, unless you are going to aim to attract a part of the market you have not attracted before.

If you are thinking of preparing publicity material you will have to do this in consultation with the partnership, but this should not stop you putting forward suggestions about the sort of material you can use. Brochures are effective and can be displayed in your reception and given to clients and to advice agencies. If you do produce your own publicity material keep the style simple, clear and unambiguous, and try to avoid sexist traps such as assuming that all solicitors are male or that all single parents with children living with them are female.

Without expanding into the field of buying commercial advertising space, small posters for display in local advice agencies and on community notice boards can have quite a good impact.

On your printed material, give the name(s) of the staff for whom an enquirer should ask because this makes the firm seem much more approachable. Clients often prefer to consult a solicitor of their own sex. If, within your firm, there are matrimonial lawyers of each sex then this is obviously an advantage.

IMAGE

Think about your image; the way you and your firm come over to the client. This is one of the themes of this book and I do not think that it can be overemphasised. Your client will judge you by all sorts of things, but the one thing that will have the least impact to start with is the quality of your work, which your client, unless he is very experienced in matrimonial litigation, is not in a very good position to judge.

Image is not just superficial. If you care enough to take trouble to present yourself to your client as efficient, caring and practical, this should be apparent from the way you approach her and the case. It is not unethical to make the most of this and use it as a selling point. There is no virtue in false modesty in this context.

DRESS

Although it may seem a frivolous topic, do not underestimate the importance that attaches to the way you dress and your general appearance.

The aim, as always, is to be professional. What this means can depend largely on what sort of firm you practise in and what is expected of you by your employers. In some firms there are clear, if unwritten, rules. In some firms, for example, there is a 'no trousers for women' rule. In the absence of any such rules you need to think about what sort of image you want to present. There is a school of thought among lawyers working in publicly funded practices that you should dress down rather than up because you do not want your style of dress to intimidate your client. Whatever your own personal preference, bear in mind that you represent a profession and clients may have particular expectations associated with that. This means that you should be fairly conventional and formal, and as smart as you can afford. But, above all, be clean and tidy.

If you succeed in looking professional, you will look like a 'proper' lawyer to your client who will have confidence in you. You may also find that looking professional is useful when you are dealing with other people such as the police or housing authorities, especially if you are not very experienced – formal clothes may give you confidence and more authority.

For men a dark business suit is uniformly acceptable. Women have to decide whether a dark suit or a more relaxed but smart style is appropriate. Nowhere is this more important than in court. If you are acting as advocate, you should be suitably clad. Keep to formal dark clothes. Avoid dramatic jewellery. I have known a judge refuse to hear a woman advocate who was wearing dangling earrings of a fairly modest nature. Even if you are not the advocate and you are 'sitting behind' counsel, you should moderate your dress. It is noticed by the judge, and casual dress is regarded as indicating a lack of respect for the court. You should also ensure, if you are sending someone else from your firm to court, that they are appropriately dressed.

Remember that, as well as your profession, you represent your client who should have the best possible chance to put his case to the court and have it heard as impartially as possible. You should not do anything, however small, which might upset that. Your client will notice, and will draw comparisons between you and the other lawyer. If you are properly dressed it will be a matter of pride for her and boost her confidence in you.

SUMMARY

- Give plenty of thought to your image and publicity.
- Build up a network of contacts for referrals.
- Develop publicity material.
- Your image should be that of a member of a responsible profession.
- Aim to dress appropriately.

Chapter 15

WORKING WITH YOUR SECRETARY

If you are a solicitor who is young, newly qualified or new to a firm, the relationship with your secretary can be a difficult one to get right. Your secretary is often older than you, more knowledgeable about the law and may initially be paid more than you. She may have been at the firm longer than you and have established her own routine. If you handle the situation clumsily, it may drive you both to tears or drink. But with consideration on each side, you should be able to establish a long and enjoyable working relationship. How do you achieve this?

LEARN FROM YOUR SECRETARY

If your secretary is older than you and has more experience of the law or the firm than you do, make the most of this. Find out what she knows and put her advice to good use. Take the time to find out from her what the office practice and procedures are and what the general atmosphere in the department is like.

Secretaries are, in my experience, an invaluable source of information on office politics. They can guide you about partners' fads and foibles. They can also alert you to bad moods and inappropriate times to interrupt your boss.

INVOLVE YOUR SECRETARY

A good secretary is more than merely a typist, and you must remember this when delegating your work. It is no good lining up piles of typing without explaining to her what you are trying to achieve and the background to the matter. Tell her about the clients and their circumstances and your feelings about them. You do not have to set aside a lot of time for this. Discuss with her what you want to achieve and how to achieve it as you go along.

If you have a file on which there is a lot of important work, keep your secretary involved with it. Make sure that she knows why it is important and, if it is urgent, why it is urgent. If a client needs really sensitive handling, make sure that she knows and knows why. If you are involved in a legal procedure which is outside the normal run of things, tell her what you are doing and why, and sketch in the legal steps for her. This makes it easier for her to follow the course of events and, if the client is talking to her instead of you, she will not sound uninformed and uninterested.

If you want to set up a new office procedure, or change your way of working, talk to her about it first; see what she thinks and whether she has any useful comments. You do not want to burden her with extra administration if she cannot see any useful purpose to it, otherwise you will meet with resistance which will make it difficult to put it into practice, and you will both end up frustrated.

ENCOURAGE YOUR SECRETARY

Be aware that your secretary may wish to advance her own career and perhaps attain a higher qualification or achieve the status of assistant rather than secretary. If so, do what you can to encourage and help her; and if you are able to turn her into your assistant, it will be to your mutual advantage.

WORKING AS A TEAM

Working with your secretary as part of a team is not mere altruism, it has a hard practical purpose. The aim is that you and your secretary should work together, each contributing your own skills to the work. As you will not be available to your clients all of the time you will need to rely on your secretary as backup. Your clients need to have confidence in you and your secretary; to know, for instance, that they can leave messages which will be passed on in a coherent form. You need to have some of the weight of routine matters taken off your shoulders so that you can concentrate on dealing with more difficult problems. A reliable secretary with whom you have a good relationship and who understands what you are trying to achieve is a godsend in these circumstances.

It may be appropriate to find out about your secretary's home life and what sort of person she is. Again, this is not something you will find out all at once, it will take time and is a two-way process. Enquire about her family and how the weekend went. This does not merely make the working atmosphere more cordial, it makes you more approachable. It means that if your secretary has any problems which spill over into her work, she will discuss them with you and you can make appropriate allowances.

COPING WITH IMPERFECTION

Inevitably, in some cases, you will not get the sort of backup you need, and no amount of initiative on your part is going to make things much better. It takes time and patience for you and your secretary to get to know each other, and it requires a lot of effort on your part.

This is not a problem to be faced alone. Indeed, your relationship with your secretary is not something which should ever be dealt with by you alone. It is important for you to keep the other people in your department (particularly your senior colleagues) aware of how you work together. If there are problems, discuss these with them so that they are aware of the difficulties. You need to give a realistic assessment of whether problems will get better in time or whether you think they are becoming insuperable.

IMPROVE YOUR OWN OFFICE TECHNIQUE

Most people are bad at dictating: they do not enunciate clearly; they wave the microphone around; they turn off the machine too quickly and cut off the ends of words; they forget about punctuation and forget to explain on which file they are working. Try listening to yourself on tape for a while. If you spot these faults, try to correct them. Ask your secretary if there are things which you could do to improve the quality of your work to help her.

You can do all sorts of things which make her life easier. For instance, flag the things that you want copied as enclosures. Keep a list with each tape of what is on it and in what order. This actually helps you both as it is easier to find files that are not in the cabinet.

One of the most vital things to get right is a true sense of what your priorities are. Many people do everything at a rush, they tell their secretaries that each item is a really urgent piece of work and must take top priority. If you do this you lose all sense of perspective and nobody takes you seriously. If something really is top priority make sure that you make this clear and do everything you can to help get it out on time. For instance, you can help with the photocopying or faxing of documents while your secretary is typing. Where there are genuine deadlines, make sure that your secretary is aware of them.

SUMMARY

- Where appropriate, learn from your secretary.
- Involve your secretary so that you work as a team.
- Respect her individual needs and feelings.

- Monitor difficulties and discuss them with others.
- Improve your office technique.

USEFUL ORGANISATIONS

These are organisations which may be of help to you or to your clients. You may find it useful to give some of these names and addresses to your clients direct and get them to contact the organisation if they feel it would help them.

Al-Anon Family Groups UK & Eire
61 Great Dover Street
London
SE1 4YF

tel: 020 7403 0888
fax: 020 7378 9910

e-mail: alanonuk.@aol.com
website: www.hexnet.co.uk/alanon/

Provides help and support for the families of alcoholics.

The Foundation for the Study of Infant Deaths
Artillery House
11–19 Artillery Row
London
SW1P 1RT

tel: 020 7222 8001
24-hour helpline: 020 7233 2090
fax: 020 7222 8002

e-mail: info@sids.org.uk
website: www.sids.org.uk/fsid/

Provides help and support for parents who have been bereaved by the sudden death of a child.

Child Poverty Action Group
94 White Lion Street
London
N1 9PF

tel: 020 7837 7979
fax: 020 7837 6414

e-mail: staff@cpag.demon.co.uk
website: www.cpag.org.uk

Publishes an invaluable guide to welfare benefits.

Gingerbread
7 Sovereign Court
Sovereign Close
London
E1W 3HW

tel: 020 7488 9300
fax: 020 7488 9333

e-mail: office@gingerbread.org.uk
website: www.gingerbread.org.uk

A self-help organisation for one-parent families. It has a network of local groups which may be helpful to your clients.

Institute of Family Therapy
24–32 Stephenson Way
London
NW1 2HX

tel: 020 7391 9150
fax: 020 7391 9169

e-mail: ift@psyc.bbk.ac.uk
website:
www.instituteoffamilytherapy.org.uk

Provides course and information for families and professionals working with them.

National Association of Citizens Advice Bureaux
Myddelton House
115–123 Pentonville Road
London
N1 9LZ

tel: 020 7833 2181
fax: 020 7833 4371

website: www.nacab.org.uk

Provides useful publications and other advice for your clients, including debt counselling.

National Council for One Parent Families
255 Kentish Town Road
London
NW5 2LX

tel: 020 7428 5400
fax: 020 7482 4851

e-mail: info@oneparentfamilies.org.uk
website: www.ncopf.org.uk

Provides useful publications and advice.

Jewish Marriage Council
23 Ravenhurst Avenue
London
NW4 4EE

tel: 020 8203 6311
fax: 020 8203 8727

e-mail: jmc@dircon.co.uk

Provides particular advice on obtaining a *Get.*

National Childbirth Trust
Alexandra House
Oldham Terrace
Acton
London
W3 6NH

tel: 0870 444 8707

e-mail:
NCTInfo@nctrust.swinternet.co.uk
website:
www.nctpregnancyandbabycare.com

Provides help and support for mothers, particularly new mothers. It has a network of local groups both pre- and post-natal. Some clients with babies may find this helpful.

NSPCC
National Centre
42 Curtain Road
London
EC2A 3NH

tel: 020 7825 2500
fax: 020 7825 2525

e-mail: infounit@nspcc.org.uk
website: www.nspcc.org.uk

ParentlinePlus
Unit 520
Highgate Studios
53–79 Highgate Road
Kentish Town
London
NW5 1TL

tel: 0808 800 2222

website: www.parentlineplus.org.uk

Provides advice and help for parents and step-parents about all stages of a child's life.

Reunite
PO Box 24875
London
E1 6FP

Advice line tel: 0207 375 3440
Admin tel: 0207 375 3441
fax: 0207 375 3442

website: www.reunite.org.uk

Provides advice and help for parents and lawyers on child abduction.

UK College of Family Mediators
24–32 Stephenson Way
London
NW1 2HX

tel: 020 7391 9162
fax: 020 7391 9165

e-mail: info@ukcfm.co.uk
website: www.ukcfm.co.uk

The professional standards-setting watchdog and public information providing body for family mediation in England, Scotland, Wales and Northern Ireland.

Relate: National Marriage Guidance
Herbet Gray College
Little Church Street
Rugby
Warwickshire
CV21 3AP

tel: 01788 573241

website: www.relate.org.uk

Local branches of Relate are in the phone book. It has a very good on-line bookshop.

Solicitors Family Law Association
PO Box 302
Orpington
Kent
BR6 8QX
DX: 86853 Locksbottom

tel: 01689 850227
fax: 01689 855833

e-mail: mary.ianson@sfla.org.uk
website: www.sfla.co.uk

Women's Aid Federation
PO Box 391
Bristol
BS99 7WS

National Domestic Violence Helpline tel:
08457 023 468
Admin tel: 0117 944 4411
fax: 0117 942 1396

e-mail: wafe@wafe.co.uk
website: www.womensaid.org.uk

INDEX

References are to page numbers.